Education Program
Newsweek

Essay writing for High School Students:

A STEP-BY-STEP GUIDE

Third Edition

A *Newsweek* Education Program Guide for TEENS

KAPLAN

PUBLISHING

New York • Chicago

Editorial Director: Jennifer Farthing
Senior Editor: Ruth Baygell
Editor: Eric Titner
Production Editor: Caitlin Ostrow
Production Artist: John Christensen
Cover Designer: Carly Schnur

Published by Kaplan Publishing, a division of Kaplan, Inc.
888 Seventh Ave.
New York, NY 10106

Printed in the United States of America

November 2006
10 9 8 7 6 5 4 3

ISBN-13: 978-1-4195-5215-1
ISBN-10: 1-4195-5215-5

Kaplan Publishing books are available at special quantity discounts to use for sales promotions, employee premiums, or educational purposes. Please call our Special Sales Department to order or for more information at 800-621-9621, ext. 4444, e-mail kaplanpubsales@kaplan.com, or write to Kaplan Publishing, 30 South Wacker Drive, Suite 2500, Chicago, IL 60606-7481.

TABLE OF CONTENTS

Section IV: Journalism

ACKNOWLEDGMENTS

This book has its roots in the hundreds of educational resources produced by the *Newsweek* Education Program. Since the 1970s, the NEP, as we call it, has supplied millions of students with tools to help them make the most of their experience with *Newsweek*.

NEP materials include poster-sized wall maps and resource units focusing on social-studies issues, English Language Arts concepts, and even life skills. A weekly teacher's guide helps educators plan their use of each week's issue. A website, www.newsweekeducation.com, allows the program to post up-to-date classroom material.

The primary author of this book is Thom Ronk, a former resource manager of the NEP. A seasoned English instructor, Thom has taught in several states, as well as in Saudi Arabia and Egypt. He has been selected as Senior English Language Fellow, as part of a U.S. government program to build Indonesia's English-language curriculum.

Contributing to the effort were the Michigan-based team of veteran educators Richard F. Bandlow and Joan K. Yehl, longtime writers of NEP curricular material. Maureen B. Costello, the circulation manager for the NEP, and Kenneth J. Paulsen, the resource manager, provided editing assistance and support from *Newsweek*'s New York headquarters.

The NEP includes a network of consultants and contributors from throughout the country. Among those whose efforts were consulted in the preparation of this text were Helen Finken, Robin Cherry Porter, Renee Hobbs, Michael Lee, Cynthia Benjamin, Catherine Gourley, Lynn Truppe, and Julie Weiss, Ph.D.

Lastly, this book salutes the many people who have contributed "My Turn" columns to *Newsweek*, as well as the magazine's staff of professional journalists, whose outstanding efforts have provided shining examples of top-quality writing.

INTRODUCTION

One of the most important skills expected of high-school graduates is the ability to write clearly. Writing clearly means thinking clearly. When it is done successfully, you show precision of thought, whether for the time-honored cover letter attached to a resume, the personal essay for a college application, or an email stating your position on a controversial subject. Masterful writing can open doors for success in life.

Too often, students are able to grasp the basic skills needed to document ideas, yet they aren't able to easily apply their own personal style and signature. The goal of writing isn't to recapitulate a topic, it is to write with poise, power, and flair. Strong writers elicit emotional responses. They explain. They persuade. And they impress.

Such writing looks easy, but in fact it requires a great deal of thought. After years of experience working with teachers in the high-school and college classrooms, the *Newsweek* Education Program staff compiled many insights, ideas, and lessons about the art of writing. As such, the focus of this book is on using the conventions of writing in a context of creativity.

Many of the essays in this book are taken from "My Turn" columns. A weekly feature in *Newsweek*, "My Turn" essays afford an individual—famous or not—the opportunity to write about a topic of personal importance. They demonstrate the power of both rich, highly detailed writing and simple-yet-eloquent description. They show how a catchy introduction can hook in readers right away, and how a smartly assembled conclusion can leave them thinking.

Additionally, once a year, to promote the importance of writing in high school, *Newsweek* and Kaplan, Inc. sponsor the Kaplan/*Newsweek* "My Turn" Essay Competition, where high school students can win up to $5,000 for college. Several of those essays are included here, too. You'll see numerous examples of how other students turned words on a page into original and compelling stories. And in keeping with that theme, we have included "Your Turn" exercises throughout the book, so that you can practice firsthand what you learn here. Remember, good writing doesn't happen overnight. It requires applying what you learn and refining your knowledge at every step.

The final section of the book focuses on journalism, *Newsweek*'s greatest strength. Examples from the award-winning magazine help provide a blueprint for the most basic forms of news writing. Topics such as interviewing, accuracy and objectivity are discussed in depth, with clear-cut examples.

As the offerings throughout this book are timeless, it is hoped that this book will serve as a reference. When you find yourself searching for the right words to conclude your essay, you can flip to the appropriate chapter for guidance and inspiration.

Section I

DEVELOPING YOUR WRITING SKILLS

CHAPTER ONE

What Makes an Essay Good?

Many of us appreciate the arts, but it might be difficult to explain why we think a song or painting is good. The work affects us; it produces a positive—maybe even a negative—response. Yet, we may not feel prepared to discuss its various harmonies, rhythms, lyrics, colors, or brush strokes. We just know it has moved us.

Similarly, we might appreciate good writing, even if we can't articulate precisely why it is good. If we feel we understand the message and it provokes in us some type of emotion, it has succeeded at its job.

What makes an essay good? The answer is simple: It engages, moves, or provokes you as a reader. Certainly a good essay will be well-written and polished. But more important, it will appeal to you in some way. It might anger you or it might fascinate you, but either way, your interest has been piqued.

While most essays have a particular purpose—anything from giving insight into human behavior to expanding one's knowledge on a topic—in some cases their goal is to just entertain. At the very least, a good essay is thought-provoking.

A good essay usually comprises one or more of the following elements:

- Originality
- Enthusiasm
- A new way of looking at old views
- Clear and well-developed presentation of a topic
- Assertion and proof that something is true

The flip side of these characteristics is easy to see. A poor essay:

- Merely restates views already stated elsewhere
- Contains tired clichés and overly simplistic vocabulary
- Includes irrelevant details
- Is unclear, unorganized, or boring
- Contains a lot of filler information and padding that is of little consequence to the argument

HIGHLIGHTS OF AN EFFECTIVE ESSAY

So, what makes an essay unique and strong? First, it has a catchy lead-in that includes a clear idea of your theme. Frequently, you'll find this in the first paragraph, though it might also be developed over a few introductory paragraphs.

Second, an effective essay contains vivid images, descriptions, and personal reflections. It may even include direct quotes to add to the veracity and flow. Depending on your purpose for writing, use of the word "I" is acceptable. Of course if the essay is a journalistic piece, where personal opinions are unwarranted, that doesn't apply, but if not, it is perfectly acceptable to speak in the first person. Writing with a first-hand perspective will add the personal touch readers are looking for. Just be careful not to use *I* in too many sentences.

Last, an effective essay concludes with a "kicker." Whether it reframes the main point or whether it poses an open-ended question, the kicker leaves the reader with "food for thought." An emphatic ending is absolutely necessary if you want readers to feel satisfied; it will ask them to consider future ramifications or developments on the topic at hand.

A GOOD ESSAY MODEL

Following is an example of a good essay. Though the author remains faithful to the basics as we traditionally see them—catchy introduction, developmental body, and thought-provoking conclusion—she nonetheless uses "writing freedoms" to express herself.

Why Teachers Are Not 'Those Who Can't'

Naturally, I began teaching for the money. And the prestige. Who wouldn't want to stand around at cocktail parties listening to some puffed-up acquaintance on a six-month consulting stint drone "Yeah, I mean teaching is great and all. But what will you do next?"

Shortly after completing my student teaching last fall, I applied for a summer job outside the field of education. The interviewer lit a cigarette and reviewed my résumé. "Phillips Academy. Very good. Princeton! Good schools you've got. Magna cum laude. Thesis prize. Teaching experience: English. Teaching?" She looked up from the paper. "But you have such a good degree! Why waste it teaching?"

I would like to say that nobody has asked me this before. That up until this point, I've had no need to defend my ambition. The truth, of course, is bleaker. So bleak that I am always ready with a response.

"Who would you rather have teaching your children?"

The interviewer sat back and took a long drag. "Well, I never thought of it like that," she conceded.

We live in an age when people seem to lament the state of public education in the same breath that they dismiss teachers as "those who can't." I cannot count the number of times a well-meaning acquaintance has assured me that I am qualified to do other things besides teach. That, by implication, I don't have to teach.

In fact, I want to spend my life teaching. I love teaching. And ritzy degrees aside, I don't think I will ever feel qualified to do it as well as I'd like.

I feel extraordinarily blessed to have been called to a profession in which I am always learning. It is grueling, exciting, gratifying work. As a student teacher in New Jersey last fall, I looked out at my high-school students and saw a field of possibilities. I looked at their clunky boots and spiked hair and adored them.

Naturally, there were downsides. On bad days, I felt I was preaching to a swarm of gnats. Yet as wretched as my students could be, it's been far more distressing to be told by adults that I have wasted my degree.

There are notable exceptions. Fellow teachers have been nothing but kind, witty and encouraging. Without a fiercely funny, intelligent mentor teacher who believed in what she was doing, I never would have survived my student teaching. Many parents with children in the public-school system are deeply invested in recruiting and retaining gifted teachers. Yet there are people both inside and outside this public-school culture who continue to wrestle with assumptions about who is and isn't teaching, often arriving at troublesome conclusions: that teachers are poorly educated, ill suited for high-powered jobs, unwilling or unable to have more glamorous careers.

Though it is decidedly unglamorous—I spent all three months of my student teaching exhausted and encrusted with chalk—teaching is deeply rewarding. In my classroom, there was nothing more exciting to me than witnessing a student write first a good sentence and then a good essay. Yet as victorious as I felt when a student nailed down a provocative thesis, employed a stellar verb or gracefully wove textual evidence into his or her paper, I was even more gratified to hear that I had touched a student personally. "She was the only teacher who didn't question my blue hair and understood the meaning of my having it," one student wrote in an evaluation. "I think you will be a great teacher someday," one of my more challenging students told me as I passed back his essay, "because you always make me feel like I'm doing good." I look

6 forward to the day when teachers are as rewarded outside the classroom—with both higher salaries and greater respect—as they are within.

Students, not teachers, may be the greatest beneficiaries of increased respect for educators. If insinuations that teachers are

7 unqualified for other careers upset educators, these notions alienate students. I remember one afternoon proctoring in-school suspension. Eager to chat after a morning of enforced silence, a tall, gangly boy asked: "You a student teacher?"

"Yes."

"Where from?" he inquired, his words reverberating off the dusty linoleum.

8 "Princeton," I responded.

"Princeton University?" he asked, flashing a broad smile. "Damn! What are you doing here? I mean, you could have been like a doctor or a lawyer or something!"

"I'm here because I want to be here," I said, smiling at his sudden animation. "Don't you think you deserve good teachers?"

"You know I deserve only the best," a sullen boy in the far corner cracked, raising his head up off the desk. As humorous as I found the moment, I could not help wincing at his irony.

—Emily Moore, *Newsweek*, April 3, 2000

This essay is especially effective because it links the author's personal experience to a large social context. The introduction (section 1) brings us immediately to the scene of a personal experience, and the language grabs our interest. Section 2 contains the author's point. Not only do we understand her personal position, we also understand its link to a big picture.

Sections 3 and 5 are personal reflections: They use details to define, support, and expand on what has been experienced. These details help us to see and feel the experience. Sections 4 and 6 are the big-picture links, using details to connect the experience to a larger social theme. This way, the author ensures she is appealing to a broad audience.

Sections 7 and 8 conclude with a kicker. They leave us with a clear understanding of the author's intent, and they reinforce that intent by illustrating a personal example.

THE PROCESS OF WRITING

Good writing doesn't happen overnight. It involves a process. That process—five steps that begin with prewriting and end with proofreading a final draft—will force you to go through the revision required to produce a polished piece of work.

The five-step process is intended to be done in linear order; that is, each step should follow the previous step. Each phase of the writing process builds upon the work done prior, so it's important to keep that momentum going. That said, the writing process is indeed flexible. Though you'll start out moving through it in order, there's no reason you can't jump back and forth.

Let's say you have finished your first draft. Now you want to go back to prewrite a bit more before moving on to the next step of *sharing*. That would be perfectly acceptable. As you work on each step, you'll think of ways to modify your work—adding, deleting, or reworking ideas—so it's logical that you'd want to go back and forth between any two steps. Above all, though, remember that no matter what sequence you use, you'll have to go through the five steps in some form. No skipping allowed!

Step 1: Prewriting

You discover you have something to express. Any one of a number of prewriting strategies can help get you going: freewriting, brainstorming, clustering, mapping. Discover your ideas at this stage; don't edit your thoughts or limit your ideas. Nor should you be concerned with grammar or spelling.

Step 2: Writing a First Draft

You begin to develop and form your idea. Here is where you begin to shape your vague thoughts into more concrete ones.

Step 3: Sharing

You seek out others for feedback. Whether it's a classmate whose opinion you respect or your older brother who has been through this before, ask them for a reaction to what you're writing. If you'd rather not share your entire first draft, at least bounce some ideas around. The benefits of sharing ideas with others are immense.

Step 4: Revising into a Second Draft

Using the feedback you have received, you'll now rewrite your essay. If you can leave your essay alone for a few days before returning to it, that will help, too. Though this is the time to pay more attention to grammar, your focus is still your meaning—your purpose for writing in the first place. If the essay as a whole does not flow, no amount of perfect grammar or spelling can help.

Step 5: Editing into a Final Draft

Once you have gotten a solid draft on paper, the rough edges need to be smoothed out. Read your essay aloud—to yourself or someone else—from beginning to end. Or ask someone whose opinion you respect to read it again for comments. Does it flow? Is any explanation missing? Are there open-ended issues that need elaboration? Are there grammatical or spelling errors?

Take one last proofread through for stray errors before handing your work in. Now, sit back and wait for the feedback and evaluation: It's precisely from evaluation that you will learn new directions for your writing, so you should welcome it!

THE UNTRADITIONAL ESSAY

We're all familiar with the traditional three-part essay: the introduction, which includes an engaging lead and theme statement; the body, a few paragraphs long with a main idea; and a conclusion, which sums up and expands on the main idea. Typically, each paragraph within the essay expresses its own idea.

The problem with this type of traditional setup is that it can be less than engaging. Though it's the most clear-cut format in terms of helping you organize your thoughts, it doesn't allow for a more creative approach to your presentation. It tends to be dry and even routine. And, at its worst, it can oversimplify the argument.

Moreover, not all ideas fit well into this format. Magazine articles and editorials, for one, are classic examples. College-application essays and other personal essays are yet other examples. The goal here is to master the art of writing a standard-type essay, and once you have done that, you can expand your style to "bend the rules." First learn the blueprint, then go on to apply a more creative touch. That way, you uphold the true goal of writing: to express yourself.

APPLYING TO COLLEGE?

Writing is a core skill for success in college and beyond. As such, the makers of the SAT and ACT, which have traditionally not included writing portions, have added short essays.

SAT: The SAT includes a mandatory 25-minute essay. You will be asked to take a position on an issue and support it with reasons and evidence. Given the short amount of time, you are not expected to turn in a polished essay, but rather a coherent first draft.

ACT: The ACT has an optional 30-minute essay. You should decide whether to complete the essay based on the requirements of the institutions you are considering.

ESSAYS FOR THE SAT AND ACT

The SAT and ACT essays require you to write on demand, so you must remember to budget your time. It is so important that we will say it again: Budget your time and plan out how you will write each paragraph. You don't want to be writing away in the middle of your essay only to hear, "Stop. Put your pencils down."

SAT

The SAT essay is a 25-minute writing assignment as part of a 1-hour writing section, which also includes multiple-choice questions about how to improve sentences and paragraphs, and how to identify errors in diction, word usage, etc.

You are given a writing prompt and asked to support or reject a position on an issue, using examples from your own life.

- Grammar will not be overriding factor in determining the essay score.
- Handwriting will not be judged (unless it is entirely illegible).
- Graders will first look at what has been done well before looking at what has been omitted.
- The essay will not be judged by its length.

ACT

The ACT essay is a 30-minute writing assignment as an optional component. You should decide whether to take the Writing Test based on the requirements of the institutions you are considering. Each postsecondary institution will make its own decisions about whether to require the ACT Writing Test.

CHAPTER TWO

Choosing a Topic

Students are frequently overwhelmed by the task of how to get started on their essay. Naturally, you need a topic. If your topic has been assigned in class, you're home-free. But if the topic is left for you to decide, what may seem like a daunting task lies ahead.

How might you approach picking a topic? A topic isn't just a fact, it's an angle on something. Here are some things that might help you stir up some ideas. Consider the following scenarios. Perhaps:

- Something is not what it appears to be
- You feel strongly that a status quo needs changing
- Something is unclear or even contradictory
- You have been disappointed by something and want to propose an alternative approach
- You are upset by a new ruling or decision and want to explain why

There are two things you must first do to frame the topic that you choose: Understand your audience and know your purpose. Once you have clarified these two things, narrowing down a topic will become an easier task.

UNDERSTAND YOUR AUDIENCE

Before you do anything, you must establish your audience. When we speak of audience, we are referring to not only the person who will ultimately read your essay. Audience means *target* audience; that is, those who would get the most from your ideas. By thinking of your audience, you can put your entire focus in context and eliminate straight away certain options for approach.

Some writers are afraid to focus on a specific audience. They feel that by doing so, the essay will be too narrow. But consider the consequences of taking the opposite approach: If your essay speaks to everyone out in the world, it won't have an angle. Of course, this doesn't mean that only target readers would want to read your essay—in fact, you should anticipate anyone reading it—it's just that by writing with your target audience in mind, you will be creating a more refined, focused piece of work.

In writing, you always want an edge. Without a target reader in mind, you're more likely to go off on tangents and lose focus. After all, when you try to please everyone, you end up pleasing no one.

If you have been given a specific writing assignment, start by looking at key words in the directions. Often they can help you figure out for whom you are writing. If you have to select your own topic, you'll have to give it more thought.

Look at the following sample audiences, and consider how your writing would change for each. It should become clear that your style would be different for each context.

- Are your readers professional/technical in the designated topic or are they laymen? Are they familiar or unfamiliar with the topic?
- Do you know their approximate age? Are they fellow students or are they older individuals with more life experience?

- Will readers need research and statistics to be convinced of your position?
- Is the reader in a position of formal authority?

So just how can knowing your audience help you begin to write? The short answer is that it will help you focus on what types of material you need to include. After all, some readers will be more accepting of a certain style than other readers. Some approaches are just not appropriate for certain audiences.

More specifically, knowing your audience will help you determine the following:

- How formal or informal to be
- How much technical language you should include
- How much detail to include
- How many statistical facts to include

UNDERSTAND YOUR PURPOSE

In the same way that your audience guides your topic, so too does your purpose. If you are writing an essay that compares and contrasts two things, your purpose will be different than if you're writing a college-admission essay. In the latter case, in your need to persuade a search committee to accept you, the essay would have an entirely different feel.

The first thing you need to do is to streamline your topic. To do this, clarify your intent. Are you writing to:

- Persuade? (persuasive writing)
- Describe? (descriptive writing)
- Share? (personal writing)
- Tell a story? (narrative writing)

Once you are clear on your goal, you should then determine who will be reading your essay. If the readers are experts in a certain field, then you'll probably choose highly focused and specialized topics. If they are classmates and peers, you'll need a broader perspective with a more conversational tone.

Think about how the purpose may be different for each of the following types of essays:

1. A letter to the editor of your local newspaper

   Purpose: to give an opinion or reaction to an article

2. A college-admission essay

   Purpose: to allow a search committee to review your credentials in relation to the school's student body

3. A letter to your state senator

   Purpose: to state your views on an issue

PREWRITING

Once you are clear on your audience and purpose, you must go through the exercise of prewriting. Prewriting is the creative phase that allows you to uncritically come up with ideas and material. Anything goes here, and your goal is to jot down whatever comes to mind. This process will eventually lead you to home in on a specific topic—broad but not vague, narrow but not confining. If your topic is too broad, your essay is bound to be either overloaded with details or inadequately argued. In short, you are looking for a narrow topic that has broad appeal.

Prewriting is a type of creative writing that's done to generate ideas. It's the time when you get your creative juices flowing. If you prewrite effectively, you should be able to discover topics and get your ideas started.

Let's look at an example of good writing and then work backward. We'll start with a finished essay, and then later examine the types of prewriting the author may have used.

Imagine you're an ordinary guy; someone who classmates teased for not being the best-looking guy in the class. Before long, you began to lose confidence in yourself based on what others thought. What would you do? The student below chose to become involved. He developed confidence and thrived.

You Can Call Me the Silver-Tongued Frog

I can't remember the first time the bullies called me Kermit. Or Froggy. Or Toad. It has become such an integral part of me that I can't imagine myself without the nicknames.

It's not easy being ugly. OK, not ugly. That's too harsh. Not facially endowed. What else can you call a guy who resembles an amphibian? People say you shouldn't judge a book by its cover, but among teenagers, the cover is what sells the book. I watched from the sidelines as my more attractive friends matched up and broke up without a care. For me, one glance from a girl was enough to feed my heart, which was shrunken from deprivation like a hunger-stricken stomach. I'd lie in my room, listen to Sister Hazel's "Change Your Mind" and swear it was about me: "If you wanna be somebody else ..."

At the beginning of my senior year of high school, I joined the mock-trial team. I needed a better way to spend my time than idling in front of my computer trying not to think of what my best friend was doing on his date with his girlfriend.

At the tryouts, in order to gauge my speaking skills, one of the lawyers who would coach the team looked me in the face and asked, "What do you think of the HIV epidemic in Africa?" Somehow, I stammered out a comprehensible answer. Surprisingly, I was awarded one of the six coveted attorney positions, while the rest of my 19 teammates were relegated to witness or clerk roles.

It was clear from the start that our training would be intense. One of the lawyer-coaches put it bluntly: "At work we charge 500 bucks an hour. We're with you guys at least 10 hours a week. You do the math. Now you want to shut up and listen?"

At every practice, the coaches would cruelly criticize our every mistake and call us everything short of complete idiots. Our opening statements were too short, our direct examinations were too long and our cross-examinations just plain stank. Then, just before we'd break down, they'd build us back up by showing us how much we had improved. Before long, we were flexing our mental muscle like true lawyers.

After our two months of training, the first competition rolled around. Before we entered the county courtroom, one of our coaches offered us some not-so-gentle encouragement: "Winning's not everything. It's the only thing."

When I walked to the podium in my suit to stand before the real-life superior-court judge and examine the "witness," a new sensation grabbed hold of me. It took me a minute to realize that it was confidence, a feeling I had never fully experienced, definitely not while conversing with a girl or sitting alone at a party. At the end of the trial, I gave my closing argument. I forget exactly what I said that made the audience, and even the other team, stand up and applaud. I just remember smiling so much that it hurt, especially as the judge singled me out as a "silver-tongued devil."

The next month seemed the shortest of my life, as my team turned in a whirlwind of amazing performances. Before we knew it, we were in the sweet 16, the elite group that remained from the original 64 teams. Three rounds later, we advanced to the final match to determine who would go on to the state championships.

The opposing team was as polished and impressive as a real dream team of lawyers. They countered all of our normally impressive arguments with even more impressive arguments of their own. As I got up to give what I thought would be my last closing statement of the year, I told myself to relish every second of it. After this, it was back to the real world, where my speaking skills were of little value to my superficial peers. I practically cried during the best closing I ever gave.

I actually did cry when, after I finished, the judge announced that my team had won and the room exploded in a roar of celebration. I hugged my co-counsels to the brink of suffocation, then rushed around congratulating the rest of my teammates. One of my coaches heartily shook my hand and admitted with a grin, "Even I was impressed."

Then I heard it. "Kermit!" I whipped around to see who had teased me. My best friend stood in front of me, beaming. To my surprise, he had come to watch me compete. "Jason," he said, "I've never heard such an articulate frog."

The team began to chant, "Silver-tongued frog! Silver-tongued frog!" In that moment I realized that I was no different from teenagers everywhere who struggle to be accepted; I won the struggle because I learned to accept myself. In that moment I was actually proud to be an amphibian. That moment was beautiful.

—Jason Shen, *Newsweek*, July 8, 2002, First place winner, Kaplan/*Newsweek* My Turn Essay Competition

Why might Shen have chosen this particular topic? Was he inspired or provoked? Do we think he first wrote solely for himself in a journal or did he know right away that he wanted to make a statement to a larger audience? What other ideas must he have thought about before deciding upon this one? Did he simply formulate his idea once he learned of the writing competition, given that there was a well-defined purpose and audience?

Shen clearly had a range of options for discovering and developing his ideas. As writers, we all do.

Freewriting

Shen may have discovered his topic through freewriting. Freewriting is when you write as quickly as you can for a set period of time. You ignore grammar, spelling, and punctuation, and instead, focus on a set topic or whatever comes to mind. Edits come later, once your ideas have been organized. You immediate goal here is to discover ideas—to reveal what's inside of you. Often the thesis you are trying to pinpoint will become apparent after a freewriting exercise.

Often when we write, we expand on what others have found or said. With freewriting, you want to focus on what *you* have found to be true. The key here is to write continuously without stopping. Don't think too much about your ideas; instead, write down anything that comes to mind. Once you hone your freewriting skills, you'll see that you have lots to say on a variety of topics—including yourself. It doesn't matter if your thoughts are unformulated and freeform: This is the first step to generating ideas.

As you begin to freewrite routinely (e.g., daily in a writing journal), certain topics are bound to resurface. After all, we all have key issues we think a lot about, and they are going to come through in your writing. Don't ignore these signs: These feelings are what you want to pick up on and clarify in your writing. They're what will make your essay unique.

To freewrite, you must:

- Write quickly for at least 10 minutes. Push yourself, even if you think you have nothing more to say.
- Write freely, without correcting grammar, spelling, or punctuation.
- Write without stopping to erase or cross out a word or mistake.
- Write as fast as you can, without worrying about neatness.
- Write without reading what you have written.
- Write continuously, even if what you're writing may seem disconnected.

You might find that you get stuck a few minutes into your freewrite. Think of something totally offbeat to stir your creative juices. Try coming up with a rhyme word for the last word you wrote and going from there. Try taking a totally new approach on the subject. Try writing about what you wish you were otherwise doing with your day. But whatever you do, don't stop writing! If you stop writing, you'll break the flow of ideas.

You might also want to consider using some tools to help you freewrite: a photograph, a meaningful personal item in your room, or a favorite article from childhood.

Brainstorming

Let's look back at Shen's essay. In thinking more about how he generated ideas, he may have tried brainstorming. Brainstorming incorporates many of the freewriting guidelines, though it's less sentence-structured. Brainstorming is when you make a list of ideas surrounding a topic. Once the list is developed, you group, organize, add, and eliminate ideas as you decide they support your topic—or not.

Brainstorming helps you to gather the facts and experiences you already know about your subject. It's a way to map your ideas. To brainstorm, you must follow this formula:

- Write the topic in the center of a sheet of paper and the purpose of the assignment at the top.
- Using single words and phrases, write down a list of everything you can think of that relates to your topic. That includes experiences, knowledge, facts, and examples.
- Do not judge your thoughts. Let your mind be creative. Later, you'll select the best ideas.

After you've made your list, you'll need to group your ideas and develop a topic or theme statement.

Here's how Shen might have brainstormed his topic:

Being Teased in High School
Cried
Bullied
Upset
My nicknames: Froggy, Kermit, Toad
Lacked confidence
Loneliness, left out
Didn't share with my parents
Watched my friends date girls while I was too afraid, shy
Silver-Tongued Frog
Trial Team tryouts
Awarded attorney position
Built my confidence
"$500 bucks an hour"

Using Inquiry

How might Shen have developed his ideas? He may have used a question-and-answer approach. The basis of inquiry starts with a question, and follows with an answer or explanation. Journalists use inquiry for most of their writing, at least in the prewriting stage.

To use inquiry, you must answer the questions:
- Who?
- What?
- Why?
- Where?
- When?
- How?

As in any writing assignment, it's best to choose a subject you are familiar with, the way Shen did. Your observations, ideas, and values should make up a large part of your writing.

SELECT AN ARGUABLE TOPIC

Present one idea in your essay, but don't make your argument one-sided. Make sure you include valid criticism and details that challenge your thesis or give it depth. If you don't, your argument might sound too simplistic.

Clustering

Clustering is another good way to narrow in on a topic. It's a way of thinking with the help of a diagram. More precisely, it helps you decide how much you have to say on a particular topic, and whether those ideas are in fact related.

Let's say you know you want to write about the *environment*. Clearly, this topic is too wide in scope; there are hundreds of approaches you could take. Thus, you need to refine your angle a great deal more. Clustering can help you do this.

DO YOU ENJOY LOOKING AT MAPS?

If you tend to think visually, chances are you'll find clustering useful. With this "visual map," there's no set linear organization. Rather, ideas go in all different directions.

To cluster, you must follow this formula:
- Start with the subject or topic in the center of a page. Circle it.
- Jot down new ideas as you think of them, and link them to the central circle with lines.
- Keep drawing lines out to link connecting ideas. The goal here is write down every word or phrase that comes to mind when you think of the topic word, forming connections between them.

Think of clustering as a five-step process:

Step 1: Eliminate inappropriate ideas.
If you are writing to inform, eliminate those ideas that are persuasive. If you are writing to persuade, decide how much material you'll need to satisfy the information needs of your audience.

Step 2: From the remaining ideas, narrow your topic.
Choose a topic that isn't too broad or too narrow in focus. Review the limitations of time and length for the assignment.

Step 3: Identify your strongest details.
Highlight them in a different color ink or marker.

Step 4: Identify those details that are minor or have the weakest significance to your purpose and audience. Eliminate them by drawing an "X" over them.

Step 5: From the remaining information, write a summary or "thesis" that states your topic.

REMEMBER USING TIMELINES IN YOUR OLD TEXTBOOKS?

If you're writing about something that's happened in sequence, write out your own timeline to help you keep track of your progression.

When you're done clustering, you should be able to look at your diagram to see which idea paths are workable for your essay.

The goal of clustering is to help you choose your topic. Try to follow a path that leads far out from the center of the diagram; the best topics tend to explore the outer branches of the cluster.

Following is an example of how one student clustered her ideas after brainstorming on the topic of teenage driving habits. Her thesis? All teenage drivers should be issued restricted licenses for at least two years.

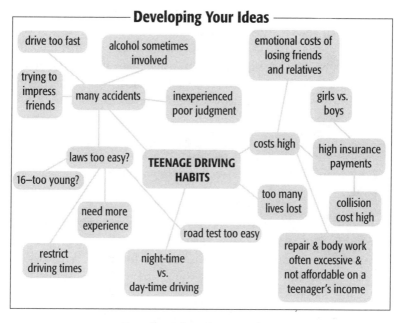

Developing Your Ideas

- drive too fast
- trying to impress friends
- alcohol sometimes involved
- many accidents
- inexperienced poor judgment
- emotional costs of losing friends and relatives
- girls vs. boys
- laws too easy?
- 16–too young?
- costs high
- **TEENAGE DRIVING HABITS**
- high insurance payments
- need more experience
- too many lives lost
- collision cost high
- restrict driving times
- road test too easy
- night-time vs. day-time driving
- repair & body work often excessive & not affordable on a teenager's income

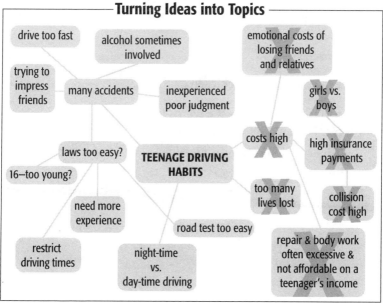

Turning Ideas into Topics

- drive too fast
- trying to impress friends
- alcohol sometimes involved
- many accidents
- inexperienced poor judgment
- emotional costs of losing friends and relatives
- girls vs. boys
- laws too easy?
- 16–too young?
- costs high
- **TEENAGE DRIVING HABITS**
- high insurance payments
- need more experience
- too many lives lost
- collision cost high
- restrict driving times
- road test too easy
- night-time vs. day-time driving
- repair & body work often excessive & not affordable on a teenager's income

So how do you turn your creative idea-building exercises into a topic? Look at what you've written, underline the points that jump out at you, and see if there's a thread. Then, try to write a sentence that links the various points and suggests a direction. Using that sentence, start a new freewrite or a new brainstorming session, for instance. By narrowing things down, your topic will slowly begin to reveal itself.

YOUR TURN

Try this brainstorming exercise. But first, go grab an egg and a piece of paper.

Write the word *egg* at the top of the paper. Examine the egg and list everything that comes to mind. Next, break the egg on a plate and begin adding to your list. What else comes to mind? When you've exhausted your ideas, review what you've written. Your list may look something like this:

egg	free-range	breakfast
chicken	unbleached eggs	Easter
fried	scrambled	birds
over-easy	poached	

Which came first, the chicken or the egg?

Your next task is to arrange the words in groups, and finally, write your topic. Perhaps you came up with:

- "An evolution conundrum: Which came first, the chicken or the egg?"
- "Free-range eggs may be more expensive, but they may save your life."
- "The importance of breakfast has changed significantly in the last 30 years."

CHAPTER THREE

Mapping Your Ideas

Once you have chosen a topic, you can start mapping your ideas. Mapping ideas means seeing them visually on paper, which in effect makes it easier to understand specific relationships.

What types of visual associations does mapping help you make? On the most obvious level, two ideas may be related in their function or design. Perhaps one idea is a subset of another idea. Or one idea explains or challenges another idea. Regardless of the relationship, it helps you to define a central theme and to clarify in your own mind how each additional idea fits within that context. This is the stage where you are exploring what you will put—and not put—in your essay.

Before you begin to map, restate aloud the intended purpose for the essay. It might seem unnecessary and even silly to do, but don't underestimate the value of this exercise: If you have a clear sense of purpose, you'll better be able to control the direction of your writing. That is, you'll have an easier time selecting the important details and rejecting the unimportant ones.

The simplest tools for beginning to think through your essay are:

- Guided Freewriting
- Venn Diagrams
- Organizing Your Thinking (Idea Chart)
- Narrative Outlines

GUIDED FREEWRITING

Guided freewriting is freewriting on a specific topic. A more focused task than regular freewriting, it requires you to have some sense of how you feel about a topic or what you know concerning it. It's a good way to get over writer's block—and you'll be surprised at how many ideas it can generate.

FREEWRITE AT THE COMPUTER

You may wish to freewrite on the computer. If you do this, darken the screen a bit so that you discourage yourself from reading what you write. The important thing is to write without stopping.

Just as you do when you're freewriting without a focus, don't stop writing—even when you think you have nothing more to write. Pick one aspect within your topic area that you'd like to develop, and for five minutes, write continuously on that one idea. Write whatever comes to mind. Then, do it again for another focused item within the topic area.

Remember: You don't want to create a bulleted list of ideas here; you want full, flowing sentences. If you're really at loss for how to start, try using a prompt such as, "I remember when . . ." It doesn't matter whether what you write makes sense—no one else will see these notes—so be creative! Write whatever you'd like.

Eventually, after you have done several short freewrites on subsets of your topic area, you'll be able to weave a theme through your ideas. Underline the ideas that seem to come together. Pick out the ones that seem substantial and interesting. Are there two groups of ideas that can be compared or contrasted? Is there one overriding idea that defines much of the material you've jotted down? Don't worry too much that you're making a final decision; you're not, and you'll revise this as you continue the process. But at this stage, you need to get the entire argument moving forward.

VENN DIAGRAM

As you probably know from high-school math, a Venn diagram shows overlapping circles that display relationships between sets. In the same way, a Venn diagram can be a useful organization tool in essay writing. Used at the planning stage, it is a very simple yet direct way of streamlining material.

Venn diagrams are helpful when you are presenting two or more views. If you were writing an opinion piece or a compare-and-contrast paper, consider using this format to help you sort out your thoughts. It can help you crystallize your line of reasoning, ensuring that all the necessary components are covered. When you can organize details visually, it becomes much easier to articulate your point.

Look at the Venn diagram below. In it, two publications—*Newsweek* and the *Washington Post*—are each presented in a circle. The characteristics they share are placed in the overlapped portion, while traits they don't share are pushed to the outside.

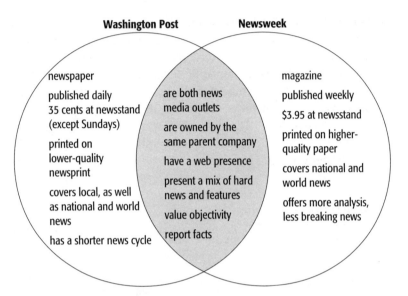

Washington Post   **Newsweek**

newspaper

published daily
35 cents at newsstand
(except Sundays)

printed on
lower-quality
newsprint

covers local, as well
as national and world
news

has a shorter news cycle

are both news
media outlets

are owned by the
same parent company

have a web presence

present a mix of hard
news and features

value objectivity

report facts

magazine

published weekly

$3.95 at newsstand

printed on higher-
quality paper

covers national and
world news

offers more analysis,
less breaking news

Not all Venn diagrams look exactly like this. The circles might completely overlap or they might not touch at all. In addition, a diagram can have more than two circles.

IDEA CHART

Another useful tool in the prewriting stage is the idea chart. Since ideas about any topic come from either your own experience and knowledge or from reference material, the idea chart helps you to combine the information.

The idea chart helps you to organize and group your ideas, which then allows you to more easily evaluate the information you have mapped. It is likely you'll discover that additional information is necessary to adequately cover your topic.

Divide a sheet of paper into two columns. At the top of the paper, write your theme statement. Label the first column *What I Already Know*, and the second, *What I Need to Know*.

In column one, list the things you know about your topic. You have already done much of this in the last step, *Selecting a Topic*. When you did the brainstorming/freewriting activities, you were listing things you knew about your topic, so build upon those lists.

To complete column two, you'll need to research your topic. This will take a little work, as it isn't always easy to "know what you need to know." Start by doing Internet research or reading, and you'll find that as you work your way through, the questions you need to ask and the things you need to identify will become crystallized.

Suppose you were given the assignment of writing a 500-word essay on the importance of wearing seatbelts. See how you might fill in the following idea chart.

What I Already Know	What I Need to Know

This information will help you clarify what you still need to gather before writing, whether it be research or interviews.

NARRATIVE OUTLINE

We're all familiar with the traditional outline that uses Roman numerals and lettered bullet points to identify major categories and subcategories. Another, more descriptive type of outline, can be helpful for developing ideas.

A narrative outline is a traditional outline but with added explanatory sentences. A skeleton of your essay, it elaborates on each point within a section. What's useful about this is that you get a more concrete idea of where your overall argument is going, and whether it makes sense as is. It's easy to lose control and write too much (having too broad a topic) or too little (having too narrow a topic), so this is a good way to gauge the accessibility and thoroughness of your presentation.

> **DO YOU THINK IN A LOGICAL, ORDERLY WAY?**
>
> If so, an outline can be useful for helping develop your ideas. You can determine what's missing and where details should fit.

A basic narrative outline is:

    My audience:

    My purpose:

    Introduction:

    Body Paragraph 1:

    Body Paragraph 2:

    Body Paragraph 3:

    Conclusion:

Underneath each header, you'll explain what will go into each section. Be sure to clarify in your own mind who the audience is and what your purpose is. Here's a sample narrative outline:

Planning My Persuasive Essay

My audience: People who are concerned about the impact of paying college athletes.

My purpose: To convince the people who are in favor of payments that a college scholarship is sufficient reward for top student-athletes, and that most colleges could not afford to pay them.

Introduction: State the situation as a whole and point out why the issue has gained momentum in recent years.

Body Paragraph 1: Point out the reasons some people feel student-athletes should be paid—that a handful of big schools could probably afford the payments.

Body Paragraph 2: Point out that the athletic departments of most schools do not earn profits, however, and cannot afford to pay their student-athletes.

Body Paragraph 3: Point out the many benefits of a college scholarship and why that is enough payment for the student-athletes.

Conclusion: Point out the high costs that would be incurred by paying student-athletes, and then pose a question to readers: Would you be willing to add hundreds of dollars to already exorbitant tuition rates to pay student-athletes who are already getting a free education?

PUTTING IT ALL TOGETHER

Once you've got all your mapped ideas on paper, it's time to start sifting through them. You are still at the stage of exploring which ideas go together and what angle you want to take.

First, you need to decide how the material naturally falls. Is there a natural division to the ideas? a natural organization? Each category of ideas should go into a paragraph. Try to connect ideas, keeping your audience and purpose in mind. Some words and phrases will naturally seem associated, while others will seem out of place with no context.

Based on how the material flows together, try to come up with an overall statement of your position on this topic. This is the thesis or main idea. This should set the tone for the rest of the essay, and will help guide you as you write. Everything else you write in the essay must somehow relate to this sentence.

Let's say you have chosen to write about a social or environmental problem. Think through the following questions before you begin to build your essay.

Step 1: What is the issue at hand?
- Identify the main issue and the angle you wish to present.
- Explain why this issue is problematic or noteworthy.
- Describe what might happen if this issue is not "corrected."

Step 2: What are the key supporting ideas and the opposing sides of the issue?
- Identify the "special-interest groups" and others affected by this problem.
- Summarize the response to this problem by each group.

Step 3: What is the best solution?
- Identify the possible solutions.
- Explain which solution is most practical and optimal for the circumstances.
- Can this solution lead to other problems?

YOUR TURN

Sometimes the best way to understand a concept is to apply it to a nonacademic subject that you're highly familiar with. In order to understand the value of mapping your ideas before writing your essay, consider what you did with your time the previous two summers, and what you plan to do next summer.

Some similarities and differences should be apparent. Whether you focus on jobs you held or vacations you took, identify what you'd like to do again and what changes you'd like to make. Pick at least two of the tools discussed in this chapter—guided freewriting, Venn diagram, idea chart, or narrative outline—and use them to organize your thoughts. You don't need to write the essay, but when you're done organizing, you should have a clear idea how you might approach such an essay.

CHAPTER FOUR

Getting Your Opening Paragraph Right

Starting off your essay can be the most intimidating part of the writing process. It's no wonder, as this is where you set the stage for the entire text. You're making your first impression, and as we all know, first impressions count. If you aren't able to draw in the reader early on, chances are, he won't go past the first paragraph.

There are two questions to keep in mind as you write your opener: First, do your introductory remarks clearly pave the way for what is about to come in the text? And second, would anyone want to read it—even those who don't have to? Stating the point and grabbing your reader's interest are indeed the most crucial things you'll need to address. Everything else is of lesser importance.

WRITING FOR YOUR COLLEGE APPLICATION?

Make sure your opening sentence is catchy. If it isn't, you're fighting an uphill battle for the attention of the admissions adviser reading it.

STATE YOUR POINT

As you probably know from your writing assignments at school, the thesis states the controlling idea of the whole essay. Whether it's one sentence or an entire first paragraph, this is the place to generate interest in your topic. Some writers will use the entire first paragraph as a "setup" to create interest and will place the thesis in the second paragraph. If the essay is a long one, this can be very effective. In other essays, the thesis, or the theme, is apparent though not precisely stated.

YOU MIGHT NOT NEED A TOPIC SENTENCE

Some types of essays–the more creative types–don't always require a concrete topic sentence or thesis statement. The goal there is to be original and follow a set line of thinking. As long as the discussion is logical and clear, the topic will be inferred from the text.

Some great essays focus solely on a personal experience, but those that seem to reach the widest audiences go beyond that. They take the personal experience and apply it in a larger context—perhaps referring to a social theme.

Read the following opening paragraph, and consider how else the writer could have approached the topic.

Fibromyalgia: Not All in Your Head

For years, Lynne Matallana couldn't wear jewelry. The pressure of a necklace or watch against her skin burned—like a blowtorch. Lying in bed under cotton sheets was agonizing. Friendly handshakes sent pain shooting up her arm. Matallana, 48, of Orange, Calif., went to 37 doctors over the course of one year before she received a diagnosis of fibromyalgia—a condition involving pain throughout the body, heightened sensitivity to touch, and fatigue. And she thinks of herself as one of the lucky ones. "Patients used to go for decades without diagnosis or treatment," says Matallana, who went on to found the National Fibromyalgia Association in 1997.

—Claudia Kalb, *Newsweek,* May 19, 2003

You are probably disappointed that the rest of the article isn't included here. That's proof of this text's strength: You're eager to read more. You want to find out more about this disease and the breakthrough that has only recently provided relief to victims.

Be aware that the author could have approached this story from others angles:

- A summary lead would have pointed out the fact that thousands of Americans struggle with fibromyalgia. Readers however, have become numb to large numbers because they're so common.

- A lead that focused on the cure might have interested science types and sufferers of fibromyalgia, but its appeal would have been limited at that point.

The personal lead, however, maximized the appeal of the story. Why?

- This introduction focuses on a regular person. The subtext of this approach is that Lynne Matallana could just as easily be you.

- Every sentence of the paragraph offers compelling, hard-to-believe facts. We immediately want to know, "How?" and "Why?" And the only way to find out is to read on.

- The description of the disease forces us to subconsciously connect with how a necklace or a cotton sheet could cause so much pain.

These are great accomplishments for an introduction. And though your introduction might not be this refined, you should strive to accomplish the same effect. Lure readers in and increase the possibility that they'll want to read every word.

Regardless of your topic, you must attract the reader's attention. That's done straight away, at sentence one. You might introduce a provocative quote. You might cite an interesting fact. You might bring in a bit of humor. You might ask a question. No matter what you do, it should be original and refreshing.

Before we address the issue of what you do want to do, let's first talk about what not to do in your introduction.

1. Don't begin your paper with, "This essay will discuss the pros and cons of studying abroad," or "I will write about when I discovered skateboarding and how it made me who I am today." Not only are these types of statements boring, they're unengaging. Show the reader what you're going to discuss, don't tell him.

2. Don't make a hollow and boring statement, such as "The world's population crisis has reached an extreme proportion." Though it might indeed be true, it does nothing to add your personal signature to the topic. These types of statements are usually unoriginal.

3. Don't state the obvious. Give readers some credit and don't bore them with facts they likely already know.

4. Don't include dry definitions, unless you're using them to compare or contrast with something more original. If readers wanted straightforward definitions, they would use the dictionary themselves.

Now, let's discuss what you *do* want to include in your introduction.

GRAB THE READER'S INTEREST

First, begin with a lead: a sentence of immediate interest. Use clear direct wording that answers the questions "Who?" and "What?" Vivid sensory details and images also spark the reader's interest.

Read the following introductions, each from different "My Turn" essays. What about them draws you in? Does the writing make you want to know more about the topic?

> I grew up a fisherman. It was predetermined. My father was a fisherman, my grandfather, and his father, too. I could tie flies before I could tie my own shoes. I could catch a feisty cutthroat trout long before a baseball, and for second-grade show and tell, I brought mounted fish instead of teddy bears. I was raised on Saturday-morning fishing shows, not cartoons, and I'm still a sucker for spinning-lure infomercials. I was outfishing my eldest brother by the time I was 9.
>
> —Ryan Grady Sample, from "Bigger, but Not Better,"
> January 11, 1999

> It was after midnight when the police came for me. I was standing in the kitchen, stunned, not sure what had just happened or what to do about it. But it all became surrealistically clear as I was led from my own house in handcuffs, bathed in flashing coloring lights. Having gone only a few hundred yards on our way to the station, we came upon more flashing lights at the scene of an accident. "See that," the cop snapped at me. "You did that."
>
> —Michael Denne, from "Learning the Hard Way,"
> November 23, 1998

I'm a loafer. A bohemian. The possessor of a $100,000 Ivy league education, which I steadfastly refuse to use. Or so I've been told. Actually, I'm a dreamer. A jet-lagged dreamer just back from a trying family get-together where, between forkfuls of lasagna and lapfuls of coffeecake crumbs, I explained to 17 family members and scores of family friends exactly what I'm doing with my life. Judging from their expressions, it's "not much."

—Danielle Kwatinetz, from "What's Your Real Job?,"
October 12, 1998

I am an orphan, but that's not what defines me. When I walk around the University of Akron campus, I look just like every other freshman—scared and confused, but filled with excitement and optimism. I do, however, face one challenge that separates me from the rest of the bunch. On July 1 the foster-care system in Cleveland cut me loose from state custody. I officially "aged out" of the system. Because regulations vary from state to state and county to county, aging out can mean turning 18 or graduating from high school. Though I ask myself the same questions as my classmates—How am I going to pay for school? Where will I go for the holidays and in the summer?—I am completely alone in making my decisions.

—Kevin Sieg, from "Growing Up a Foster Kid,"
October 26, 1998

CHOOSE VIVID WORDS

Exciting sentences bring images to life. They do so with:

- Figurative language
- Descriptive words
- Action words
- A variety of sentence structures (some long, some short)
- Use of the active voice
- Interesting vocabulary

It's not hard to see why vivid words make writing more interesting. When you include abstract generalizations, it's hard to grasp anything real. With hollow words—words that just take up space but don't really add anything of value—all that ends up happening is that the reader gets distracted from your message. Express your ideas in simple, clear, positive terms.

Let's look at the following text, a good example of vivid language.

The Tip Sheet

Road Test: Porsche GT2

One of the great perks of being the host of "The Tonight Show" is that you get to do a lot of cool things. Recently, I mentioned to someone how much I like the new Porsche GT2. Then I got a call from Porsche asking me if I'd like to drive it for a week or two. Duh! The GT2 is a cut above the already incredible Turbo Carrera. With 456 horsepower, you can drive it faster than you can read this sentence. Of course, the speed limit is 55 and it would be wrong to go faster. The GT2 is pricey, about $181,700. With a top speed of 195, it costs about a thousand bucks for each mph.

The thing I like about Porsches is that they're not big, heavy cars with giant wings that take up the highway. Because the GT2 is rear-wheel drive instead of all-wheel drive, you can drift it in the corners. A powerful two-wheel-drive car is great for doing burnouts at the Dairy Queen. And that's really what a midlife crisis is all about, isn't it?

—Jay Leno, *Newsweek*, Sept. 30, 2002

How does Leno hook us in? He uses himself, for one—his own celebrity status as a television host. We know right away that we're reading the work of a comedian with a tongue-in-cheek personality. His writing is familiar and engaging, the same way he is on TV, and his tone, with phrases such as "do a lot of cool things," and "Duh," is relaxed and humorous. In addition, his use of vivid images, along with his well-known satire ("Of course, the speed limit is 55 and it would be wrong to go faster" and "great for doing burnouts at the Diary Queen") add to the compelling Tip Sheet item.

YOUR TURN

Choose a new product on the market that you'd really like to have. Write a 200-word Tip Sheet item reviewing the product. Be sure to hook in your reader from the start and to use vivid images. After you have finished writing and revising, share it with a few friends to get their feedback. Ask them whether in fact your writing grabbed their attention and how.

CHAPTER FIVE

Great Paragraphs: Topic Sentences

Paragraphs are the foundation of writing. They are tools that help writers build ideas. Great paragraphs are created with clear, strong, active sentences that effectively express what you are trying to say. That starts with a strong topic sentence.

A topic sentence, then, could be described as the "backbone" of the paragraph. It determines the content, flow and style you want to communicate. As such, it must do the following:

- Communicate one idea
- Catch the reader's attention
- Identify what the paragraph is about
- Support the theme of the entire essay

The topic sentence for the entire essay is called the *thesis statement*. This sets forth your topic; that is, an *opinion* about a fact. It cannot be just the piece of information itself, such as *the environment*. What position are you taking about the environment?

Not every paragraph needs a clear-cut topic sentence. If you are detailing an event, for instance, it isn't essential. In that case, every sentence is of equal importance. But in most cases, particularly when you are analyzing something or promoting a point of view, a topic sentence will help focus you—and your reader—on the point at hand.

COMMUNICATE ONE IDEA

The idea of your paragraph should be stated in the topic sentence. Keep it focused on one idea—if you're too broad, you're likely to lose your reader. You don't want your reader to have to guess what the text will discuss. Even though in your mind things may be obvious, you can't assume that on the part of the reader.

Most often, a topic sentence comes at the beginning of a paragraph, though that isn't always the case. One option is to start the paragraph with a question, and answer that question in the text that follows. In that case, the answer to the question will be the topic sentence of the paragraph. Another option is to place the topic sentence at the end of the paragraph, where it summarizes its main idea. Not only is this a good way to build the suspense for your reader, it also helps to provide an easy transition into the next paragraph.

THERE'S NO RULE

Though a topic sentence is typically found at the beginning of a paragraph, don't lock yourself into a formula. You might want to present it in the middle of a paragraph–or even to lead up to it in the last sentence.

Here's an example. In this example, each paragraph begins with a topic sentence, and builds upon the idea expressed in the topic sentence.

A Different Kind of Selling Out

When John Freyer decided to unload a few of his things and go live in New York, he couldn't imagine it would come to this. Two years later he still hasn't moved to the Big Apple, but he has managed to move everything he owned. Freyer put it all up for sale online, every single possession, and then used the $6,000 he made to visit his old stuff all over the country. "I've become amazed by the history and genealogy of objects," says Freyer, who's engaged to the woman who bought his kitchen table.

His new book, "All My Life for Sale" (Bloomsbury), chronicles one man's junk-peddling odyssey in which everything had a price— old phone books, used mouthwash, even sideburn clippings in a plastic bag and a set of false teeth that a museum paid $27 for. The tape from Freyer's answering machine went for $15.50, a handwritten list of phone numbers fetched $14.50 and a brick that was bought for $3 was mailed to London for $35. (A handful of items found the dump.)

A couple of weeks ago, the unlikely salesman made what he said was his final deal: Freyer sold the film rights to his idea of selling everything. With a briskly selling book and a movie deal, Freyer seems to have cashed in on his plan to sell out. But what use is money to a guy who can't seem to keep anything he buys?

—Geoffrey Gagnon, *Newsweek*, December 9, 2002

Each paragraph here provides a distinct point of information that extends *from* the previous paragraph and leads *into* the next one. The transitions are smooth. The first paragraph sets the scene by telling the basics about Freyer's mission, while the second provides details about the mission that lead to the book deal. The last paragraph tells about the subsequent movie that grew out of the book deal, and includes an amusing kicker. Each paragraph is linked to the others; together, they make a cohesive story with a logical flow.

CATCH THE READER'S ATTENTION

Good writing hinges on strong paragraphs and compelling themes. A topic sentence should catch the reader's attention and limit the paragraph to one or two main points.

Following are some useful questions to ask yourself to make sure you are keeping the reader interested:

1. Have you challenged a routine idea or presented a familiar topic in a new way?
2. Does your writing evoke humor?
3. Have you probed people's memories?
4. Have you stimulated interest in something not often talked about?
5. Have you asked a question, or raised curiosity about something?

Look at the following essay, keeping the above questions in mind.

Talented, Like Totally

Fifty years ago it took a talented adult novelist to capture the wayward voice of a generation in "The Catcher in the Rye." These days, kids just do it themselves. Or at least one kid has. Nick McDonell was 17 when he wrote "Twelve" (Grove Press), a nihilistic novel appearing in bookstores next week. McDonell is no J. D. Salinger. But he's smart enough to know that. Ask him if he doesn't think the characters in his book aren't a little, ah, thinly drawn, and he quickly agrees: "My characters are caricatures of themselves." He could've argued that the teens he writes about are disaffected prep-school louts from the Upper East Side of Manhattan with too few brains, too much money and way too much access to all sorts of drugs. In other words, they're supposed to be so shallow that they're hard to tell apart. Instead he does the stand-up thing and tells the truth: "I'm not good enough yet to do full-blown psychological portraits." What he does know how to do is establish a mood (completely creepy) that he sustains to the bitter, blood-soaked end. And he knows how to make you keep turning pages—his book generates a nasty narrative undertow that writers twice McDonell's age would pay dearly to pull off. He makes it look so easy that people talk less about his talent and more about the fact that his father is Terry McDonell, editor of *Sports Illustrated* and good friend of Morgan Entrekin, publisher of Grove Press. Which raises the reasonable question, would any of this have happened had Nick McDonell not been born into the right family with the right connections? Probably not. Is his novel nevertheless an arresting debut? Absolutely. Nepotism works best when it doesn't need to.

—Malcolm Jones, *Newsweek*, July 1, 2002

The author catches our attention by challenging the established idea that teens can't write strong literature, evoking humor, and by raising the issue of nepotism in the publishing world.

IDENTIFY WHAT THE PARAGRAPH IS ABOUT

A good paragraph communicates what will be discussed. It doesn't make the reader guess at the topic. In order to accomplish that task, the topic sentence should serve to direct the order and content of the rest of the paragraph. Supporting sentences should present enough detailed information to support and explore the main idea stated in the topic sentence.

A strong topic sentence can be rendered ineffective if the information surrounding it is weak or irrelevant. To develop your topic sentences into intelligent, stimulating paragraphs, consider the following:

- Examples provide evidence for the main idea. True stories, or anecdotes, add human interest and credibility.

- Facts provide concrete details. They may include statistical data.

- Reasoning provides the arguments for a writer's point of view. Quoted material may be used.

When focusing on paragraphs, notice that each sentence relates directly to its topic sentence.

SUPPORT THE THEME OF THE ENTIRE ESSAY

In addition to introducing your main idea, a topic sentence at the paragraph level also serves to connect the paragraph that preceded it. Make sure you allude to the topic discussed in the previous paragraph; that way, your ideas will flow smoothly from one paragraph to the next. Once you do that, you'll want to introduce a new topic in the current paragraph.

INTRODUCE NEW MATERIAL SMOOTHLY

When using a topic sentence as a transition from the previous paragraph, make sure it introduces the new material adequately.

Read this article about health in the United States, paying particular attention to how each paragraph builds on the ideas of the previous paragraph and contributes to a cohesive article.

Is Our Society Making You Sick?

Americans are obsessed with health. Just look at today's magazines, TV shows, Web sites, self-help books—and where we put our dollars. As a country, we make up about 4 percent of the world's total population, yet we expend almost half of all the money spent on medical care. We should be pretty healthy.

Yet I have always been amazed at how poorly the United States ranks in health when compared with other countries. When I began medical school in 1970 we stood about 15th in what I call the Health Olympics, the ranking of countries by life expectancy or infant mortality. Twenty years later we were about 20th, and in recent years we have plunged even further to around 25th, behind almost all rich countries and a few poor ones. For the richest and most powerful country in the world's history, this is a disgrace.

As a physician obsessed with understanding what makes groups of people healthy, I'm dumbfounded that our low ranking doesn't raise more concern in the medical and public-health communities. Is it because experts in these fields don't want to question the role of medical care in producing health? Does our focus on diseases—including the search for risk factors, cures and specific preventive answers—stop Americans from looking at what would really keep us well?

Research during this last decade has shown that the health of a group of people is not affected substantially by individual behaviors such as smoking, diet and exercise, by genetics or by the use of health care. In countries where basic goods are readily available, people's life span depends on the hierarchical structure of their society; that is, the size of the gap between rich and poor.

How can hierarchy affect health? Consider the feelings that predominate in a hierarchical situation: power, domination, coercion (if you are on top); resignation, resentment and submission (if you are on the bottom). Compare them with feelings in an egalitarian environment: support, friendship, cooperation and sociability. Studies with baboons in Kenya and macaque monkeys in captivity, both of which feature strong hierarchical relationships, show that high-ranking animals are healthier than those lower in the pecking order. Human population studies show additional findings. The death rate from heart attacks among middle-aged men is four times greater in Lithuania than in Sweden, which is much more egalitarian.

We can learn something by looking at countries that do well in the Health Olympics. In 1960 Japan stood 23rd, but by 1977 it had overtaken all the others in the health race. Today, at No. 1, Japan has a life expectancy on average three and a half years longer than the United States'. Twice as many Japanese men as American men smoke, yet the deaths attributable to smoking are half of ours. Why? After the second world war, the hierarchical structure of Japan was reorganized so all citizens shared more equally in the economy. Today Japanese CEOs make 15 to 20 times what entry-level workers make, not the almost 500-fold difference in this country. During their recent economic crisis, CEOs and managers in Japan took cuts in pay rather than lay off workers. That the structure of society is key to well-being becomes evident when we look at Japanese who emigrate: their health declines to the level of the inhabitants of the new country.

Did this health-hierarchy relationship always exist—is it part of human nature? Archeological records from burial mounds and skeletal remains indicate that human populations were relatively healthy before the advent of agriculture. The development of farming allowed food to be produced in quantities and stored, enabling some to live off the efforts of others—a hierarchy. With agriculture, health declined, nutrition worsened and workload increased.

Why has the medical community, as well as the popular press, essentially ignored these findings? I suspect that part of the explanation lies in Americans' "cradle to grave" relationship with the health-care industry, which represents one seventh of the U.S. economy.

> If equality is good medicine, then what can be done to improve Americans' well-being? Our primary goal should be to reduce today's record gap between rich and poor. Prescriptions for such "structural medicine" might include a tax on consumption rather than income, or increased support for public transportation, schools and day care, all of which would reflect a change in how the population shares in the economy. We must put our eyes on a new prize: doing better in the Health Olympics. The best prescription for health is not one we will get from doctors.
>
> —Stephen Bezruchka, M.D., *Newsweek*: My Turn, February 26, 2001

YOUR TURN

Write a short paragraph using the following prompt. Be sure you include a strong topic sentence followed by supporting sentences.

- Identify a historical figure you would like to have lunch with and explain why.

CHAPTER SIX

Great Paragraphs: Developing Your Ideas

Writing an effective paragraph is like building a house: You need to begin with a solid foundation before you add the finishing touches. Not having a solid foundation can result in some serious consequences: Both the building—and the paragraph—can crumble.

A paragraph is a group of related sentences that expresses a single idea. Your job as a writer is to communicate this idea clearly. Well-written paragraphs share these important characteristics:

- A great paragraph has unity. That means it sticks to the subject. It doesn't wander by jumping from subject to subject without any apparent purpose. All sentences are related to one single idea.

- A great paragraph has coherence. That means the paragraph's ideas are presented in a logical order and are linked together in a way that makes it easy for the reader to follow your train of thought.

- A great paragraph has adequate detail. That means it has enough supporting details so your reader can easily understand the paragraph's main idea.

The same principles make a great essay. That is, the paragraphs, collectively, should have unity and coherence, as well as detail, when linked to the essay's thesis.

UNITY

Unity is essential at both the paragraph and the essay level. Each paragraph should, in some way, refer to the topic at hand. This is not to say that there should be only one idea per paragraph, but one thing is certain: all ideas should touch on your theme.

The following essay illustrates how unity can sustain the interest of readers. Throughout your reading, note the purpose of each paragraph, and how the author sticks to the topic.

The Newspapers Tell Only Half of the Story

Whenever I pick up a newspaper, I see articles about the dismal state of race relations in America, and I feel as if I have once again entered a long, dark tunnel where I'm surrounded by anguished faces and heavy hearts, and where no one dares speak of anything positive. The truth is, relations among the races are far better than many thoughtful and concerned Americans give themselves credit for. We are without a doubt a prejudiced nation, but there are countless numbers of us who refuse to give in to our own worst impulses.

But everyday kindnesses that cross the color line don't make good copy like churches' being burned or a black man's being dragged behind a truck in Texas. When Sen. Trent Lott said publicly that our country would have been better served if arch-segregationist Strom Thurmond had won the presidency in 1948, the story gained so much momentum that Lott was eventually forced to resign. I'm glad he did, and that the story forced us to ask ourselves how our society could have allowed this individual to rise to such an elevated post.

These examples of bigotry and ignorance prove that racial tension is always bubbling underneath the surface of blacks' and whites' interactions with each other, but I don't think that should cause us to lose hope. The fact is, most people choose each day to treat each other with respect; we'd live in a state of chaos otherwise. These acts of tolerance may not sell newspapers, but they are what ultimately moves us forward.

My understanding of how far basic fairness can take us came early on in the form of Miss Daily, my eighth-grade teacher. Though she was only five feet tall, she was a very powerful lady, the queen of her domain. I was one of three black students in the class, but she made me feel equal to every other student in the room. She didn't do this by delivering searing diatribes on race relations; she simply treated me like everyone else. She never gave even a hint that her students' race mattered to her. Regardless of our color, we all had to adhere to the highest academic standards. What she demanded of one, she demanded of all. Eventually I, too, became a teacher, and when I encountered students whose backgrounds were racially and ethnically diverse, the memory of Miss Daily helped me to judge my young charges on nothing more than the quality of their work.

In my personal life, I'm surrounded by decent people who continue to choose kindness over bigotry. One white neighbor built some steps for me this summer and has yet to ask to be paid. Another white neighbor repaired my mailbox after some kids smashed it with a baseball bat. He never mentioned it to me; I discovered his generosity on my own.

I remember another example of the brighter side of race relations that happened just before my best friend died in November 1992. Though terminally ill, Melvin was always hopeful that he would see the sun rise for one more day. Two weeks before he died, I visited him and his wife in his hospital room. Mel was especially pleased because on this particular evening, he was being entertained by a young white guitar player who came to the hospital twice a week to play for cancer patients. Mel, whose dark skin was blackened even more by the chemotherapy that ravaged his body, listened with rapt attention to the jazz music, his favorite.

While Mel was absorbed in the music, I was thinking of something else altogether. I was marveling at the scene—a young white male playing for three black friends with whom he had not the slightest acquaintance. This, I thought, was at least a partial answer to our country's racial misunderstandings. We had discovered a common thread, in this case music, and were enjoying it with equal passion. Loving what is shared leaves little room for loathing what is different. In that room and among those four individuals, there were no rules, no regulations, no quotas, no affirmative-action concerns—just one caring musician, a loving wife and a lifelong friend transcending race to bring joy to a suffering man.

Moving beyond race, like all human involvements, always comes down to caring. To think beyond race is commendable; to act beyond race is to take a real step toward a more equal society. We'll know we've made progress when we can automatically look past the color of a person's skin and focus on his or her value as a human being. I believe we're getting there, one small act of kindness at a time.

—Wes Carter, *Newsweek*: My Turn, January 13, 2003

Did you notice how each paragraph sticks to one point, and how all the paragraphs connect to the essay's thesis? Let's break it down for clarity.

Thesis: Race relations are better than the nation is given credit for.

Paragraph 1 (Introduction): Newspapers don't tell the whole story about race relations.

Paragraph 2: Sensational cases grab headlines and national attention.

Paragraph 3: We must realize that these cases are rare exceptions, not the norm.

Paragraph 4: I learned the value of colorblindness at an early age.

Paragraph 5: People I know have clearly learned the same lessons that I have; life is better as a result.

Paragraph 6: My best friend's death provided an enduring image of a colorblind world.

Paragraph 7: Music was the common bond we shared, not the color of our skin.

Paragraph 8 (Conclusion): More needs to be done, but progress is being made.

The author develops unified paragraphs and coherent supporting sentences for each idea, many of which are descriptive, adding necessary details and examples. In the end, each paragraph is interesting to read.

More concretely, how can unity be achieved?

- **Make sure each paragraph has a purpose—a point—that can easily be discerned.** This can best be accomplished with a topic sentence. Look at sentence one in paragraph five. "In my personal life, I'm surrounded by decent people who continue to choose kindness over bigotry." It introduces the paragraph's main idea and signals what is to follow—in this case, examples of such decent people. In other paragraphs, the topic sentence is not explicitly stated in one sentence, but the topic is clear in that the sentences focus on one idea.

- **Use each sentence to advance the paragraph's main idea.** The author does not stray from his subject—he stays with the topic at hand. The result? Your interest is sustained.

- **Use each paragraph to advance the essay's main idea.** Note the sturdy framework of the outline in the previous section: Paragraphs 1–3 introduce the topic with a clear premise; paragraphs 4 and 5 provide supporting evidence; and paragraphs 6–8 provide strong concluding evidence that affirms the author's initial premise.

- **Revisit each paragraph several times, rewriting where necessary.** The fine-tuning process results in paragraphs that are focused, and an overall essay that stays on message. The essay's overall unity is apparent.

COHERENCE

Coherence is the glue that keeps an essay together, and it has two dimensions: first, whether your text makes sense to the reader, and second, whether it flows smoothly. In terms of making sense, try to include some good examples when you make a point. Follow them up with some discussion to show your understanding of the matter. Make a connection right away between your topic sentence and the evidence you have to support it. You're going from a general statement to a specific illustration in a few brief sentences.

As for cohesion and smooth flow, think of how you might unfold a story. (Your essay, in whatever form, is indeed a story!) While you know all the details of your argument, you cannot, and should not, assume that the reader knows any details. When he reads, your train of thought must be apparent. There should be no guesswork involved.

There are things you can do to maintain coherence in your essay. You can repeat key words or ideas throughout. You can refer to things discussed in previous sentences and paragraphs. You can make abstract ideas more concrete by using examples or specifics. You can explain the implications of something on which you have speculated.

Keep in mind that things do not always have to be connected in a positive way. Comparing and contrasting or making valid criticism are effective ways to bridge ideas.

Transitions

Many writers confuse their readers by not connecting the content of one paragraph with the next. This is a grave error in essay writing. You don't want your reader to have to figure out where your text is leading; you want it spelled out. If it isn't, your reader may end up going back a few times to reread what she has read; that is, trying to figure out what one idea has to do with the next.

All effective writing contains transitions: the words, phrases, and sentences that connect ideas and supporting information. Among other things, a good transition can help to add information; provide an example; show a contrary point; elaborate on something; show cause and effect; or illustrate a sequence of time or space.

At both the sentence and paragraph level, transitions are critical: Each sentence must flow into the next, and each paragraph must flow into the next. Some transitions are simple and are understood in just a word or two: *in spite of, therefore, consequently, moreover, nonetheless.* Others are frequently used without having to think about their meaning, such as *first of all* or *finally.* Yet other transitions are full sentences, such as, "Though that may be the case this year, it wasn't always that way in previous years."

A good transition is especially important at the end of your essay. When you are summing up your thoughts and bringing the argument together, you must flow smoothly into the concluding idea.

TRANSITIONS ARE A LINK

Transitions help the reader to remember what you have just stated and to anticipate what is about to follow.

Your transitions should not require too much thought on your part. If your essay is well-developed and organized in a logical fashion, the transitions should, for the most part, come naturally. If you know that the paragraphs are choppy but can't figure out how to smooth them out, go back and make sure that the paragraphs logically follow each other. Why did you place them one after the other? Explain that reason to the reader with transitions. Maybe there's a crucial element missing in this flow of thought? Maybe your paragraph would be better placed somewhere else? If you have trouble connecting one paragraph with the next, look carefully at the sequence of your paragraphs. You may not have structured your ideas in the most logical order.

The most effective way to connect ideas is to use words that refer back to the previous paragraph. Reinforce and expand upon ideas used in the previous paragraph. Don't just plug in transition words that you think will bridge two ideas. It will require more than just one word or two to connect your ideas.

While transition words are critical, too many of them will distract the reader and throw off the flow of your language. Use only those transition words that you need.

Another reason to not just throw in transition words or phrases where you think they're required is that your reader will likely be able to detect they were haphazardly stuck in. Pay close attention to the first and last sentences in each paragraph. Taken together, do they accurately reflect the main idea of your essay?

The last sentence of one paragraph should always lead smoothly into the first sentence of the next paragraph. Even if it's just one word, such as *however*, you must somehow acknowledge and build upon what you have just stated. You cannot merely go on to a new idea without transitioning, that is, linking the ideas together.

FOR A COLLEGE APPLICATION ESSAY

Admissions counselors must read thousands of student essays in college applications. When writing your college application essay, those essays that successfully–or unsuccessfully–make logical transitions will stand out. Make sure your essay flows smoothly.

Transitions help make your paragraphs read smoothly by connecting ideas and reinforcing their place in the overall essay. A sentence that starts with the word *Earlier*, for example, provides a time reference for both the current and preceding ideas, allowing the reader to keep track of the order of events. By introducing a subject with the word *However*, you're indicating that the next point to be made will rebut the previous one. The judicious use of these subtle cues ensures that your readers will follow your essay's direction:

- **To indicate time order**
  before, earlier, previously, formerly, recently, presently, by now, until, after, soon after, later, following

- **To indicate sequence**
  first, once, to begin with, initially, from this point, secondly, next, then, after that, at last, in conclusion, consequently

- **To add a point**
  also, besides, for one thing, plus, furthermore, in addition, moreover, similarly, above all, however, yet, but

- **To indicate spatial arrangement**
  under, over, overhead, below, in the background, to the right (or left), here, nearby, close to, far from, on the other side, surrounding

Keep in mind these are only a few of the many transitions you can use to construct coherent paragraphs. The more you read and write, you'll begin to notice and learn numerous others.

Paragraph Structure

It goes without saying that a paragraph is easy to understand when it is logically organized. Your reader should be able to follow your train of thought. Here are some of the most often used patterns in paragraph organization:

- **Deductive order** is when a general statement is made at the beginning of the paragraph and is followed by sentences that support it. It is used in paragraph five of the essay at the start of this chapter.

- **Inductive order** is similar to deductive order, except that the generalization occurs at the end of the paragraph. In this construction, supporting statements are given first, leading up to the generalization or main point.

- **Chronological order** is the order of time. Details are arranged in the order they occurred. Best used for narrating an incident, giving instruction, or detailing the cycle of a scientific experiment, this type of organization uses transitions such as *first, second,* and *as a result.* If you explain the steps of a process, arrange the steps in the order they should be performed.

  Example: Getting an unrestricted driver's license is not as easy as it seems. First, you need to take a driver's education class. Next, you have to pass the state's written exam. Then you have to take the road test. If you pass, you'll receive a conditional license, which will be upgraded to unrestricted status if you stay out of trouble on the road for six months.

- **Spatial order** is the order of a particular setting or place. This pattern is most often used when writing descriptive paragraphs—that is, the physical descriptions of a room or an environment. You show the reader where things are located from your perspective. Details are arranged from left to right, top to bottom, etc. It is up to you to choose the order, with the goal of transporting the reader to the place being addressed.

  Example: The U-shaped dorm room affords both students a measure of privacy, with one student on the left side and the other on the right. When guests walk in the door, they must turn to go to either side, because a pair of large closets serves to neatly divide the room.

- **Order of importance** is used in paragraphs that explain or persuade. The writer organizes the details from the most important to the least important, or the reverse.

  Example: Why do I want to go away to college? For starters, I think it would be really cool. There would be no curfew, and I could even eat ice cream for breakfast if I wanted. I'd get to meet new people and learn how to live on my own. But, most important, the education would allow me to pursue my dream of becoming a biologist.

- **Subdivision** involves enumerating points in a short list. This approach can be used to list basic supporting arguments, or to explain several aspects of an issue.

  Example: Each of my three closest friends brings out a different part of my personality. When I'm with Jessica, the class clown, I crack jokes and laugh a lot. When I get together with Steve, who plays baseball and football, we either talk about or play sports. And Randy, my buddy on the honor roll, always brings out my intellectual side.

- **Comparison and contrast** is a helpful way of explaining the similarities and differences between two subjects.

  Example: I enjoyed watching the first season of *The Osbournes* much more than the second one. The spontaneity and excitement of the first season are gone, replaced by predictable episodes and bland dialogue. In the first year, I felt like I was really peeking into the Osbournes' lives. This year, they're acting like they know the camera is following their every movement and recording their every word.

- **Posing and answering a question** is especially effective when addressing a question that is likely on readers' minds.

  Example: Do college admissions officers really read those essays we write on our applications? They certainly do. It's the one opportunity for them to see who we are, outside of all of the test scores, report cards and lists of student activities. An essay that showcases your best effort might make the difference between acceptance and rejection. At the same time, a poorly constructed or uninspired essay will send a message that you're not the right material for that college.

DETAIL

Have you ever heard the phrase, "It's all in the details"? It basically means that grand statements and ideas are meaningless unless they are backed up by details—specific examples that support your point. A credible thesis and eloquent language cannot rescue an essay that lacks detail—it's a fatal omission. Use the strategies below to infuse your essay with detail, and in the process convince readers that your point is valid.

Personal Experience

If you have strong feelings about a situation, there is usually a reason for it. Be sure to tell that reason to your readers. After all, it shaped your opinion—maybe it can do the same for them! The description of a personal experience can be a powerful tool for communicating ideas. It places readers in your position and compels them to understand your viewpoint.

Facts

Your point of view will be respected more if your essay includes factual information in addition to your opinions. It's a way of telling the reader, "This isn't just what I think—these facts support my point." Seek facts that are supplied by the highest possible authority—a government agency, a respected pollster, a research study, a university, or a seasoned executive. Just as personal experience adds one dimension of credibility to your essay, factual detail adds another.

CHECK YOUR SOURCES

Factual information will support your thesis, but be careful where you get your material. Advocacy groups, while often respected, are notorious for supplying only statistics that strongly support their views. Over-reliance on such organizations' fact sheets may weaken your argument.

Objectivity

The best way to earn a reader's trust is to show that you have been fair in your analysis. This isn't always easy to do when you have a strong opinion about a subject. But playing devil's advocate—that is, by taking the opposing side's point of view in order to reason through your argument—has its advantages. It gives you credibility—the power of which cannot be understated—by showing readers that you have conducted background research and considered other points of view before taking your stance. In other words, you've made an informed judgment, not a knee-jerk decision.

Readers respect carefully crafted criticism of alternatives—a sign that you've given thought to your position. But they'll be wary of trusting an essay rife with ridicule—a sign that you've never considered alternative views. Which type of writing would you be inclined to respect?

Analogies

Make it easy for readers to understand your points. When you're discussing a complex issue, the best way to explain it may be to compare it to something everyone is familiar with. The following text uses a perfect analogy to explain President Bush's incremental method of introducing economic and tax proposals:

> If you've ever heard the riff about how to boil a frog, you'd understand what President Bush's economic and tax proposals are all about. You don't just toss the frog into a pot of boiling water, because even the foggiest frog would figure out that something was wrong and jump out. Instead, you start with room-temperature water and boil Froggie over a low flame, so the water warms slowly. By the time the frog realizes that he ought to get out of the pot, he's cooked.
>
> — Allan Sloan, *Newsweek* column,
> "The Tax Cut Ate Granny's Check," February 17, 2003

Appealing to Reason or Emotion

Sometimes, the facts aren't enough. In the following text, the author rails against those who intentionally deplete their personal savings so that the government can pick up the cost of their long-term care. Such tactics likely cost the nation tens of billions of dollars a year, but the author knew that such statistics would bounce off most readers. Instead, she appealed to their sense of shame and ethics:

Medicaid is designed to help the truly indigent. If we steal from the federal government, or the state of California, we steal from our fellow citizens, whose taxes go up to pay for our care. Medi-Cal currently pays about $1,000 less a month than the average private patient. That means nursing homes must raise the rates for private patients to compensate.

—Diana Conway, from *Newsweek*: My Turn,
"Cheating Uncle Sam for Mom and Dad," January 27, 2003

NO JUMPING AROUND!

Don't jump from subject to subject within a paragraph. That would show lack of organization and an unclear sense of purpose.

Perspective

Conway's paragraph above also illustrates the importance of perspective. What is perspective? In short, it answers the question, "What does it mean to me?" The inclusion of perspective is another tool that allows readers to relate to the point at hand.

In another example, a *Newsweek* article on the growth of the organic-food movement begins with an anecdote. We're told at the start about a conventional farmer who bought into an organic farm because he was so concerned about the dangers of pesticides. The next paragraph, which logically followed the first, explained that the trend is growing, and listed some major companies that have joined the bandwagon. But at that point, the author focused on a question that was likely on readers' minds. The following paragraph shows how he provided perspective:

What exactly are consumers getting out of the deal? Until now, the definition of "organic" has varied from one state to the next, leaving shoppers to assume it means something like "way more expensive but probably better for you." Not anymore. As of Oct. 21, any food sold as organic will have to meet criteria set by the United States Department of Agriculture. The National Organic Rule—the product of 10 years' deliberation by growers, scientists and consumers—reserves the terms "100 percent organic" and "organic" (at least 95 percent) for foods produced without hormones, antibiotics, herbicides, insecticides, chemical fertilizers, genetic modification or germ-killing radiation.

—Geoffrey Cowley, *Newsweek*, from
"Certified Organic," September 30, 2002

YOUR TURN

Find examples in the news of three techniques often used in paragraphs to support topic sentences.

- **Examples** provide evidence and lend credibility to the idea expressed in the topic sentence.

- **Quotes** provide the reasoning needed to support an opinion expressed in the topic sentence.

- **Facts** provide concrete data to support a topic sentence.

CHAPTER SEVEN

Great Paragraphs: Communicating Through Tone

Tone is the subtle attitude you communicate about your subject when you write. As you do when you speak, you reveal a certain posture—a mood or perspective—every time you put words to paper. This is done through the kind of language you choose and your arrangement of words. This is done through punctuation and word length. And this is done with the level of confidence you show in your approach to the material.

IT'S MORE THAN JUST THE WORDS

While it's true that the tone will be dictated in part by the subject matter, it's also a function of the choices you make as you write.

Tone may be hopeful, glum, affectionate, tongue-in-cheek, devious, weighty, ironic, or dark. Whatever form it takes, it is as essential as the words in a text. Without it, words run the risk of coming across as flat and mechanical.

WHAT IS TONE?

Read aloud the sentences below, using the tone of voice suggested in parenthesis.

(*thoughtfully*)	Yes, I believe you.
(*sarcastically*)	Yeah, sure, I believe you.
(*suspiciously*)	Yes … I believe you.
(*angrily*)	Yes, I believe you!

Most likely, as you interpreted each statement, the articulation, emphasis, and rhythm of your voice changed. Perhaps your facial expression or gestures changed, too. By emphasizing one syllable or word over another, you suggest a certain meaning. By sliding your voice up at the end of a sentence, for instance, you communicate doubt or a question.

While the speaker relies on vocal and visual cues to communicate tone of voice, the writer is restricted to tools on the written page. One mark of effective writing is the way a writer incorporates his personality into the topic. A good writer's "voice" is clear but doesn't overpower the subject matter. When writing, you must rely on the effects of carefully crafted language to communicate an attitude.

NOT ALL TONE IS INTENTIONAL

Even when you are trying to write an objective text, your choices will reveal a certain tone. Ask someone else to read your essay and identify the tone. Then, revise as necessary.

How is tone communicated? It is revealed through:
- Word choice and connotation
- Choice of details
- Arrangement of words
- Pairing and repetition of words
- Choice of punctuation
- Order of ideas

If you want to convey a friendly, casual tone, you might use short sentences and paragraphs, or colloquial expressions. Contractions, too (*you're* rather than *you are*), are a feature of more informal writing, as are certain punctuation marks over others. A semicolon, for instance, as opposed to a comma or dash, can direct how the sentence should sound in the reader's head.

A more formal tone might include longer, more complex sentences, and neutral pronouns (*it* and *they* rather than *I* or *we*). It does not use contractions, nor does it address the reader as *you*. Formal doesn't mean stuffy, however. One trick might be to imagine you're addressing your best friend's grandmother: You would be respectful and polite, but you would stick to the same language you use everyday. If you want your essay to come across as thoughtful and rational, take this into account as your write.

> "Last week alone, more than 100 new human cases of West Nile were reported. The virus was detected as far west as Colorado and Wyoming, infecting 371 and killing 16 people in 20 states plus the District of Columbia. This year West Nile appeared earlier in the mosquito season—mid-June instead of August—and claimed younger victims; the median age dropped from 65 to 54."
>
> —Debra Rosenberg, *Newsweek*, "We're Not in Crisis Mode," September 2, 2002

Notice the tone in the passage above. It is factual, authoritarian, and formal, devoid of a personal opinion. Totally objective, it provides us with only the facts, and we're left on our own to decide how it should be interpreted.

CONNOTATION CAN MAKE THE DIFFERENCE

To interpret tone accurately in reading, you must pay attention to word choice and connotation. While denotation is the precise dictionary meaning of a word, connotation is the emotion a word or phrase suggests.

IMAGERY

A gloved hand, a rotting limb, a slit of frosted glass—writers of nonfiction as well as fiction use imagery to tell their stories. They create images by carefully selecting words that appeal to the five senses: sight, smell, sound, taste, and touch. These sensory details in turn help to create tone throughout the text.

Imagery can be literal or figurative. Literal images are just that— literal and clear-cut. *A slit of frosted glass*, for example, doesn't suggest any further meaning. These types of details help the reader envision the time, place, and action in the story.

IMAGES HAVE CONNOTATION, TOO

For tone to be consistent throughout a piece, the images–both literal and figurative–must echo or mirror one another.

Figurative images, on the other hand, suggest meanings beyond the dictionary definition. When Robert Lipsyte writes in The New York *Times* that Michael Jordon, Wayne Gretzky, Steffi Graf, and John Elway are "archangels of the arena," he creates a metaphor comparing two dissimilar things—athletes and the highest order of angels.

Read the passage below, paying attention to how the writer uses literal or figurative images (or both) to create tone.

Down on the Body Farm

The air smells sickeningly sweet, with honeysuckle and death. The Body Farm—the only place in the world where corpses rot in the open air to advance human knowledge—sits on a wooded hillside an easy three-minute stroll from the University of Tennessee Medical Center in Knoxville. Not everyone comes here voluntarily. The cadaver under the honeysuckle, for instance, had been shot in the chest and abdomen after a drug deal gone wrong 10 days earlier. No one knows what happened to his headless neighbor 20 feet away—a woman found floating last summer in the Tennessee River. William Bass III, 73, the Body Farm's founder, doesn't find the scene ghoulish. "I see this as a scientific challenge," he says, as maggots work efficiently on 20 or so corpses decomposing in the early autumn sun. Then Bass uses a gloved hand to lift a rotting limb.

Ask any detective. Solving a crime—from a drug-cartel hit to a garden-variety murder—often depends upon pinpointing the time of death. To do so requires the empirical study of decomposing humans; this humble site in Tennessee is the world's foremost laboratory for doing just that.

Over the years, more than 300 people have decayed on this leafy Tennessee hillside—some in car trunks, others under water, some under earth, some hung from scaffolds. Corpses of criminals whose relatives won't pay to bury them sometimes end up here. But more than 100 people, many of them academics and professionals, have signed up on their own for afterlife on the farm.

—Daniel Pedersen, from "Down on the Body Farm,"
Newsweek, October 23, 2000

The writer skillfully juxtaposes the smell of honeysuckle (sickeningly sweet) with death and wooded hillside, and an easy stroll with the image of decaying corpses. Rather than create a ghoulish or horrific tone, this visual comparison suggests that death is a part of life. The tone is one of authority and indifference rather than shock at what the body farm is.

What do you think the writer means by a "drug-cartel hit" and "garden-variety murder"? Are these literal or figurative images? *Drug-cartel hit* is quite literal—it brings a violent killing to mind. A *garden-variety murder* is more figurative. A contrast of images, it combines something living and pleasant with something violent. It is figurative in that it suggests a symbolic meaning. What kind of murder happens in a garden? Who's fighting? Lovers? Siblings? Perhaps a stranger appeared from nowhere. Quite deliberately, a figurative image is neither precise nor explicit.

REPETITION

Public speakers and writers often use repetition to persuade an audience to their way of thinking. The repetition might be a single word but it might be an entire sentence. The connotation of the words (i.e., the purpose and emotion) creates tone, while the repetition of words emphasizes authority and firmness of conviction.

In his inaugural address in January 1961, President John F. Kennedy issued a warning:

> "Let every nation know, whether it wishes us well or ill, that we shall pay any price, bear any burden, meet any hardship, support any friend, oppose any foe, in order to assure the survival and the success of liberty."

As readers, we feel Kennedy's confidence in the country and his focus on protecting liberty. The strength of his words comes in part from his use of repetition: The word *any* is used five times in a single sentence, which communicates how strongly he believes in what he is saying. And within the sentence itself, you have a repeated syntax: action verb plus *any* plus noun (*pay any price, bear any burden*).

THE HUMAN-INTEREST ANGLE

Another way to create tone is to incorporate human interest into your essay. A human-interest angle is something that creates an emotional response, telling a personal story so that the reader will relate on an impulsive level. Just as repetition is a rhetorical device for emphasis and persuasion, so too are details that trigger an emotional response. Depending on your purpose and audience, the emotion can range from joy to fear, compassion to consternation.

Newsweek writers Andrew Murr and Flynn McRoberts selected an unusual quote to conclude their story about the capture of seven escaped convicts from prison. They could have quoted one of the state police officers who made the arrest, one of the convicts, or even the news anchor who interviewed the men. Instead, they quoted Marilyn Murray, a resident of the trailer park where the convicts were living.

> "Just two days ago I'd thought of baking some cookies and bringing them over to them. Thank God I didn't."

Murray, of course, had no idea that the seven strangers who had recently moved into the trailer park were, in fact, convicted felons. Nor did she know that inside their RV were police radios, weapons, and more than $70,000, which the men had allegedly robbed during their weeks on the lam.

The visual image conveyed here injects the story with a colorful image. But it is the second half of Murray's quote—*Thank God I didn't*—that packs the emotional punch and shifts the tone of the sentence from warmhearted to cold fear. By showing how the news affects ordinary people, the writers are alerting their readers—this could have happened to you!

A HUMAN-INTEREST ANGLE CAN CREATE TONE

Focusing on how events affect people both personalizes a story and gives it credibility. This can be done by quoting real people and noticing gestures, clothing, and other seemingly insignificant details.

Read the following article describing a personal experience in the Vietnam War. The emotions are subtle yet disturbing.

The Homecoming of Chris Mead

Chris Mead sat halfway back in the bus, staring vacantly out the mud-streaked window at the wintry Michigan countryside. The trees were black and bare. A patchy snow covered the ground. The only sounds were the whack-whack of the windshield wipers and the drowsy whine of the tires on wet pavement. Mead was wearing a brand-new Army uniform, with Spa/4 insignia on the sleeves. But the war was over for him now, and he was going home.

Mead is one of the more than two million U.S. military men who have served in Vietnam and returned, and, like many of them, he came back discouraged by what he had seen of war and uncertain of what he will make of peace. He had been discharged only the day before at Oakland, Calif. It took all day before he got to the last steel cage and drew $524 in discharge pay. "Is that it? Am I out now?" he asked. "That's it," the paymaster said. Mead started out, past a huge wall painting of Uncle Sam in tears. I'LL MISS YOU, it said. Mead gave the poster the finger.

That was his farewell. He had joined the Army with six classmates from Ovoid-Elsie Consolidated High School near Owosso, Mich.; three are still in, two got medical discharges, one was killed in action. Mead himself took a lot of gunfire—"I was dead for sure a couple of times." He saw trucks blown up, kids maimed, women killed, buddies bleeding and dying. Once he saw a Viet Cong running away on the stumps of his shot-away legs. And now he was out, and no one said good-bye or good luck. There was just the "Certificate of Appreciation" with President Nixon's facsimile signature. "I extend to you my personal thanks and the sincere appreciation of a grateful nation," it said. "You have helped maintain the security of the nation during a critical time in its history."

Only coming home, you'd never know it. Elsie, Mich., is just the sort of Middle America town that used to welcome its boys noisily home from the wars. But when Mead's bus pulled into the dingy Indian Trails Bus Depot in nearby Owosso in a light snow, the only one there to meet him was his kid brother Greg, 19. They bear-hugged. "You've gotten so big, man," Chris said. "You're bigger than I am."

They got into the family car, a green 1967 Chrysler. Mead drove, out of town and across the tracks and past big red barns and herds of Holsteins and crossroads stores with Smith-Douglass Fertilizer signs. They didn't talk about the war at all. "Check it out: I'm 21 now," Mead said; he had turned 21 three days before his discharge. He asked about his bedroom, his record collection, his clothes. And girls. "I've got to scope me out a really neat chick. One I can rap with, not one who just wants to have babies. How's the girl situation?" Greg grinned and said, "They're still around."

And then they were home. A sign on the side of the barn said Orlo Mead & Sons, and an electric Christmas star glowed on top. "Mom turned on the light to let the neighbors know you're home," Greg said.

Mead pulled into the icy driveway. The whole family fumbled out the side door to greet him: his parents and Vicki, 14, Neil, 11, and Brad, 7. Mrs. Mead was having a new $300 linoleum-tile floor put down in the kitchen and was apologetic about the homecoming dinner. She had managed pork chops and gravy, mashed potatoes, green peas and pumpkin pie and a store-bought birthday cake. But Mead's ulcer was bothering him. "Wow, I wish I could eat," he said. "I'm not even interested in food any more."

—Karl Fleming, *Newsweek*, March 29, 1971

Literal images in paragraph one allow us to "see" what Chris Mead sees. Taken together, the "mud-streaked window" and the "whack-whack" and "drowsy whine" create a melancholy tone. Mead stares vacantly, as if devoid of emotion.

Yet the paragraphs that follow reveal some of what Mead is feeling. It is not patriotism. Upon being discharged, he feels a letdown of sorts ("That's it?"), and bitterness. He gives the poster of Uncle Sam "the finger." The writer gives us a human-interest angle, from an insider's point of view, not a flag-flying bystander but a real soldier, who isn't smiling, feeling like a hero. He's angry and feels betrayed. The tone is created through these insightful details of his feelings.

The writer triggers a tone of sympathy for Mead by describing the bus terminal and comparing his homecoming (where only one person, his brother, shows up) with homecomings of soldiers of past wars.

On the ride home, the conversation between the brothers focuses on interests to which other young readers can relate—music and girls. This creates the tone of youth and commonality.

The description of the homecoming supper as common fare was relevant to many Americans at that time. Mead's reaction loss of appetite isn't because he isn't hungry. At 21, he has an ulcer. Although not wounded on the outside, he is hurting inside. The writer carefully uses tone, particularly images and word choices, to challenge our preconceived notions of soldiers and homecomings, to give us a different, more realistic picture. The tone is one of compassion, yet upset, too, of the unseen casualties of war.

FORMAL VERSUS INFORMAL LANGUAGE

Call a chicken a chicken or even a fine-feathered friend, and you are using informal language. But call a chicken a fowl, and that's more formal.

Whether or not to use formal or informal language depends on two things: your audience and your purpose.

It's often quite apparent which type of language you'll need to use. After all, you use a different type of language with your friends than you do with your guidance counselor. Informal language is friendly, often emotional, even passionate. Formal language is more restrained and serious in tone. Formal language tends to use complex sentence structure, be highly descriptive, and read more slowly than informal language.

Purpose: To Inform

Articles written for newspapers use informal language so that the public will easily understand. Articles written for professional or academic journals use formal language, as their readers tend to be more technically oriented with previous knowledge of a specific field.

Purpose: To Persuade

A public debate on the death penalty requires more serious, formal language. A satirical letter to the editor about the death penalty will rely on witty, informal language.

Though informal language is intended to be relaxed, slang is often considered too informal for essay writing. Moreover, it's possible that some readers won't understand what you mean. Similarly, don't overuse clichés or colloquial phrases such as *a lot* and *really*.

> **DON'T OVERUSE *I***
>
> Even if you're writing about a personal experience, don't use *I* too often. You want to incorporate your perspectives with those of the rest of the world.

Don't be confused into thinking that formal language means using big vocabulary words or technical terms. It doesn't. Sure, using big words can make a text sound more formal, but what we're talking about here is more of an overall attitude toward the subject. Any simple text, even if it includes easy vocabulary, can take on a certain tone. It can be confrontational. It can be superior. And it can be offensive.

But whether you're using formal or informal language, stick to the active voice. Use the passive voice only:

- When you want to emphasize the object of the action in the sentence, or when it's unclear who the subject is. "Smith's plane was shot down over the Pacific."

- When, due to the length of the sentence's subject, it is easier to use the passive voice. It is better to say "The decision was made by the president, in consultation with the vice president and other top advisers," instead of "The president, in consultation with the vice president and other top advisers, made the decision."

HUMOR

If done correctly, humor can help hold your reader. It can get people to reflect on an issue in a new and refreshing way. But proceed with caution: Humor in this instance doesn't mean including a bunch of jokes you might share with your friends. It means a light-heartedness— an inventiveness—in your writing, that might include comical or amusing perspectives or twists. It might come in the form of a short anecdote, and it might come in the form of a funny quotation.

Too often, students are afraid to take chances in writing. In their desire to do the right thing, they end up editing out anything unique. Maybe it's too way out? Maybe it isn't appropriate? Unfortunately, their essays end up being stale and predictable. Safe, yes, but dry and boring as well.

It's okay to push the bounds sometimes. Adding a little inventiveness and offbeat sensibility to your essay can make it stand out. But be careful: If humor isn't something that comes easily to you in speech, chances are it won't come through in writing either. In that case, you're better off sticking to your natural style of writing. Just try your best to make it original.

Moreover, your definition of funny might not be another person's definition. If you aren't sure whether something humorous is appropriate for your essay, try it out on someone else. Try to keep your humor light, and above all, make sure it isn't offensive.

If you aren't sure whether your humor is indeed funny or appropriate, try it out on a classmate or older friend.

Take a look at the following satirical news story.

"Gore Denounces Violent Breakfast Cereals"

In the hotly contested battleground of Ohio, Vice President Al Gore slammed America's breakfast cereal manufacturers, telling a partisan crowd, "Breakfast is the most violent meal of the day."

Gore charged cereal producers with knowingly marketing their cereals to youngsters—cereals that contain barely concealed violent messages. "You don't have to be an expert to know that 'Snap, Crackle, Pop' are a subliminal version of gunfire and explosions," Gore told his audience. "The cereal manufacturers are playing tricks with our children, and I'm here to say, these tricks are not for kids."

—Andy Borowitz, *Newsweek* Web exclusive, September 22, 2000

Though the tone of this passage is serious, the wordplay (in the title and in "tricks are not for kids") is humorous. The writer satirizes politicians' concern about violence in the media by creating a preposterous scenario. Of course breakfast cereals aren't violent. But the writer is also saying that politicians aren't sincere, either, in blasting violence in the media. In fact, he believes they're doing so just to get publicity and possibly votes.

> **NOT EVERY SENTENCE NEEDS TO TRIGGER A LAUGH**
>
> Sometimes the best humorous pieces start with a serious tone and end with a humorous punchline.

Incorporating humor into an essay can be very tricky. You run the risk of sounding sarcastic or flippant. Some techniques for creating humor are:

- Exaggeration
- Silly comparison—simile or metaphor
- Preposterous story
- Sarcasm
- Wordplay

INCORPORATING TONE INTO YOUR ESSAY

How do you decide what kind of tone is appropriate for your essay? First, try to keep some emotional distance between yourself and your material. Unless you are writing a highly personal essay about your feelings or experiences, your tone shouldn't be too emotive. Similarly, don't make subjective judgments about the subject; otherwise, it might seem that you are not basing your argument on facts.

As you consider the appropriate tone for your essay, identify your subject, your audience, your purpose for writing, and your message. Also, before you begin to write, make sure you jot down the "other" perspective on your topic. That will help you to write a more objective essay and to focus on answering questions the reader might have about the subject.

In addition, ask yourself the following questions:

- How informed is the reader about the topic? Does he have previous knowledge?
- Do I need to define technical language, given the background of the reader?
- What needs to be emphasized so the reader grasps my position?
- How formal or informal should I be, given the audience?

YOUR TURN

Look at some of the emails you have written to your friends, parents, or even teachers. Can you see any difference in their tone? What makes them different? Do you use ALL CAPS a lot or smiling or winking faces, or are your words more carefully chosen? What about sentence structure and length?

The same issues apply when writing essays. Know why you're writing and for whom you are writing.

CHAPTER EIGHT

Concluding Your Essay

Writers often get stuck when they get to the task of concluding their essays. After all, there are only two options: either restate the point already made, or set out a related but new idea as food for thought. Either choice has a down-side: Run the risk of boring the reader by simply restating the main point, or open the door to a new idea that comes across as unsubstantiated.

What, then, is the best way to conclude an essay? The best way is to show the reader how to apply the new perspective you have just provided. You might prefer to close with a nice click, like the door locking shut behind you, while someone else might want to leave the reader thinking of open-ended possibilities. At the very least, an ending should provide some sense of conclusion, but also with an additional something to consider.

One thing the conclusion must do is be aligned with the introduction. Try to refer to the introductory paragraph, either by including key words or similar concepts and images. Pose a provocative question. Call for some type of action. Impart some type of warning. Just do not restate what has already been said with no substantive changes.

At the very least, your conclusion should remind the reader of your thesis/theme statement. After that, your options are as follows:

- Relate the concluding paragraphs to the opening paragraphs.
- Briefly summarize, or refer to, the most important ideas.
- Suggest or restate the larger social theme.
- Use figurative language (simile, metaphor, etc.) to enhance the point.

INCORPORATE A KICKER

How many times have you used the phrase *In conclusion* or *To conclude* for your high school assignments? This may be the easiest solution when it comes to concluding your essay, but it is far from the best solution. In fact, this is the weakest possible way you can end your essay.

You shouldn't have to state that your conclusion is a conclusion. You should be tying up loose ends by repositioning the material you have just presented. The way to do that is to include some type of twist to your argument.

Read the following variety of endings. As you do, think about what each ending does for the reader.

> Before I have children of my own, I'll use my experiences to help make good decisions about whom I choose to marry. However, if I do get a divorce, I will put my children's needs first. I will stay near them no matter what happens.

> —Nick Sheff, *Newsweek*: My Turn, "My Long-Distance Life," February 15, 1999

I failed Jordan and Emily when they needed me most. They kept her pain from me because they sensed that I would not understand. They were right. But I have changed. Now when teens come to the library, I greet them with a warm smile and kind words. I laugh at their jokes and compliment them on their clothes because I know they need adult acceptance. For some, these are the only caring gestures they will encounter all day. But my biggest contribution may be finding information and recommending books that will help them better understand their problems.

Every day I see girls who remind me of Emily, and listen to stories that are similar to hers. <u>Every day I reach out to them because now I know I can make a difference. I lost my chance once. I will not let it happen again.</u>

> —Jami Jones, *Newsweek:* My Turn, "Now I Know Too Much to Turn Away," March 3, 2003

Living in the country rejuvenates the spirit, but it also has its price. We have to guard against such hazards as Lyme disease and rabid raccoons. <u>But more worrisome than any natural danger is the weapon-toting human whose reckless disregard for the law is far more insidious.</u>

> —Denise D. Knight, *Newsweek*: My Turn, "No Hunting Here, Please," October 5, 1998

The texts above employ what's called a kicker (i.e., the underlined sentences), that is, a conclusion that leaves the reader thinking. The kicker not only provokes thought, it also leaves the reader with a clear understanding of your purpose and meaning.

While a kicker is very effective in writing, it isn't the only way to end an essay. Consider these other strategies to help you write an effective conclusion:

REPEAT A DETAIL

One interesting technique for a conclusion is to repeat a vivid detail or image used at the beginning. This chapter begins with the image of a door closing behind you. When you see the image again at the end, you're more likely to remember the beginning and grasp the main point: that the conclusion of an essay is the writer's last chance to make an impression before leaving the room.

Read the following example of one student's first and last paragraphs:

Introduction
Was it a dream? I am not certain, but is seems so real, so tangible, so familiar. I was shuffling, meandering down a warm steamy sidewalk. The sprinkler watering the concrete ahead whispered for me to jump through it, so I danced with the droplets of water and squished mud in between my toes. How little my toes were! Dripping wet, I skipped over to save an earthworm from shriveling to his death in the heat, after which I befriended a frog and deposited two fat green caterpillars in my pocket. ...

Conclusion
.... Life just is not, and cannot be reduced to, a finish line. It is a journey, not a destination. Life is about running through sprinklers and saving earthworms, so to speak. It is about what you make of it along the way, not how fast you get there. We must stop running, slow down, and listen to the voice inside. Every one contains a beauty that is aching to creep out, take a look around, and soar away.

> —Elizabeth Jean Kvach, Kaplan/*Newsweek*: My Turn
> Essay Competition, from "The Race," 2000

Notice how the author uses the technique of repeating images—*lawn sprinkler* and *earthworm*—in her introduction and conclusion. She richly describes that slow shuffle down the sidewalk in the introduction, but uses the images in the conclusion for a different purpose: to explain what's important. Repeating a detail may actually spur the reader to go back and reread the beginning and really think about the writer's point.

END WITH A THOUGHT PROVOKER

An effective conclusion summarizes your main idea and ends with a thought-provoking twist.

END WITH A FLOURISH

Make your final sentence memorable. Don't just throw any sentence together because you have run out of steam. Make it original.

Here's another example of a student's first and last paragraphs:

Introduction

Now a high-school senior, I still remember my freshman year with a shudder; it was the year my friends and I joked about as the "Year of Sleepless Nights." It wasn't that I had contracted a rare sleeping disorder or suffered from a bad case of insomnia that particular year; in fact, nothing could have been farther from the truth. I had done what many diligent students do: sacrifice precious sleep for the sake of academic success.

Conclusion

After all these experiences, I frown when I hear my classmates tell stories about their parents' pressuring them to do well in school. Sometimes I wonder if their parents understand what lengths their children go to so they can sport bumper stickers on their cars proclaiming my child goes to Harvard! If that's the case, they need to learn what my parents and I have learned: academic success means nothing if your heart isn't into earning it, and in the end, books will always fail to teach you as much as life itself.

—Jenny Hung, *Newsweek*: My Turn, from
"Surviving a Year of Sleepless Nights," September 20, 1999

Here the introduction shows the essay's main point: that, even though she achieved academic success by taking honors classes and getting straight A's, the success came at a price and ultimately did not give the author satisfaction.

The conclusion summarizes key details with general words, such as *experiences* and *pressures*. And the message is restated in the conclusion: "Academic success means nothing if your heart isn't into earning it…." Finally, the last sentence provokes thought with an effective punch line (or kicker), as the author invites us to think about how to live life: "books will fail to teach as much as life itself."

YOUR CONCLUSION SHOULD NOT:

- Introduce a new idea
- Focus on one detail in the essay
- Be a sweeping generalization

MAKE A FINAL, LASTING STATEMENT

The conclusion is your last chance to get your point across to the reader. An effective way to make sure the reader "hears" what you have to say is to make a final, lasting statement.

The following essay reflects on an incident in the author's past. We learn about what the author perceives to be a problem in American society. As you read, think about whether you are left with a clear understanding of the author's purpose and meaning.

Students Are Dying; Colleges Can Do More

U nfortunately, I am an expert on drinking and driving. As a high-school freshman in Wayland, Mass., I suffered through the death of a classmate on my hockey team who was killed in an alcohol-related crash. Two years later I attended the funeral of another classmate who died while driving under the influence. Twelve months after that a wrestling teammate returning to Wayland from a college break totaled his car in a drunk-driving accident, partially paralyzing himself and causing permanent brain damage. His father, a town firefighter responding to a 911 call, was the one to find him on the roadside near death.

After all that, I thought I knew the worst about drunk driving. I was wrong. Three years ago my brother, Ryan, a Middlebury College senior, drove 70–100 miles an hour on a rainy rural road into a tree, ending his life. His blood-alcohol level was nearly three times the legal limit. Witnesses later recounted that he was swerving and speeding on a nearby road.

It was one of the worst accidents that officers at the crash site had ever seen. The two policemen assigned to wipe Ryan's blood and tissue off the car's broken windshield found it impossible even to talk to us about the details of what they found. According to the police report, before officers could transport Ryan to the funeral home, they had to remove a small branch that pierced his permanently flattened lips.

Ryan was last seen drinking on campus at a fraternity house that was serving vodka punch. He left the party intending to drive to his off-campus apartment three miles away to pick up a toga for yet another event. He never made it home. After his death, we found out that Ryan had developed a drinking problem while away at college. But even though he drank to excess at nearly every social function, usually three to four times a week, many of his friends never realized he was on his way to becoming an alcoholic.

It turns out that one of the staff members in the student-activities office where Ryan often came to register his fraternity's parties had suspected that he had a drinking problem. And Ryan isn't the only

Middlebury student to be involved in a dangerous alcohol-related incident: in the year before his death one of Ryan's fellow students nearly died in a binge-drinking incident, saved only because the hospital pumped her stomach as she lay unconscious. Her blood-alcohol level was .425 percent.

What should we do about the Ryans of the world? I know that my brother was ultimately responsible for his own death, but in my view, college administrators can work harder to keep kids like Ryan from getting behind the wheel. But many schools have been reluctant to address the problem. Why? Perhaps because taking responsibility for drinking and driving will make trustees and college presidents legally liable for college students' drunk-driving behavior. If administrators accepted this responsibility, they might ask themselves the following questions: Should we expel students who receive a D.U.I.? Has the president of our university met with the mayor to create a unified policy toward drunk driving within our town? Have we contacted organizations like M.A.D.D. and S.A.D.D. to help us implement alcohol- and driving-education programs?

On campuses like Middlebury's, where many students own cars, administrators can use more aggressive methods to combat drinking and driving. Yet after Ryan's death his university ignored my family's request to fund a Middlebury town officer to patrol the main entry into campus for out-of-control drivers on weekend evenings. This, despite the fact that the Middlebury College director of health services informed me and my family that approximately 15 percent of the school's freshmen were so intoxicated at some point during the last year that a classmate had to bring them to the infirmary.

Why does the problem of drunk driving persist? It's not easy to solve. College students are young and irresponsible, and drinking is part of their culture. Administrators have not wanted to abolish social houses and fraternities for fear that ending such beloved college traditions would lower alumni donations.

To college presidents, trustees and all college officials, I ask that you go home tonight and consider your love for your own son or daughter, your own brother or sister. Imagine the knock on your door at 3 A.M. when a uniformed police officer announces that your loved one has died. Then go to a mirror and look deep into your own eyes. Ask yourself the question: have I done enough to help solve this problem?

The choice is simple. You can choose to be a leader and an agent of change on a controversial issue. Or you can continue the annual practice of authoring one of your student's eulogies. My family, in its grief, begs you to do the former.

—Rob Waldron, *Newsweek*: My Turn, 2000

The essay provides a clear link between childhood tragedy and adult commitment. Indeed, the author attacks colleges for ignoring the problem of binge drinking.

At the end, we are left with an imaginary scenario: "Imagine the knock on your door at 3 A.M., when a uniformed police officer announces that your loved one has died. Then go to a mirror and look deep into your own eyes." Why do you think the author chose to do this? What is the effect of the picture he painted in our minds? The answer is that he wanted to evoke an emotional response of responsibility and guilt for doing nothing.

The author doesn't stop there, though. He wants to make sure we get the message, so he chose to make the last sentence a lasting statement: "My family, in its grief, begs you to do the former." Here, *former* refers to the first of his choices: to take responsibility. And in order to add strength to his request and to make it seem more important, he uses "begs" to make it affect us even more.

MY TURN

Look back at a recent essay you have completed and ask yourself these questions. Does the conclusion:

- Repeat or refer to your theme statement?
- Summarize or touch on the important points?
- Express some meaning or context about the importance of your topic?
- Use a kicker to end?

Just remember: Whether you slam it, close it quietly, or leave it ajar and peek back in—don't forget to close the door on your essay.

CHAPTER NINE

Editing Your Work

In addition to wanting to read meaningful, interesting, and engaging writing, readers want to read clear, correct, and concise writing. You want to ensure the focus is on *what* you have to express, not *how* it is expressed. Revising and editing are absolutely necessary for effective writing.

Although error-free writing cannot outshine content, it does complement and support what you have to say. If a reader struggles to make sense of your story because there are misspelled words or a choppy paragraph, then your diligence and hard work will be lost in the fight to comprehend.

UNDERSTANDING REVISION

Revision is a major and essential part of the writing process. It means editing your words from a rough draft into a final essay ready for submission. At best, it means transforming your draft into a more polished, refined text—by adding necessary details, experiences, and images, and by fine-tuning transitions. At worst, it means rewriting entire paragraphs and rethinking your approach.

IS IT APPROPRIATE?

The writing you decide not to include may be exceptional writing. The quality of your writing isn't being questioned; as a writer you're asking if it's appropriate for your purpose. You may decide it's too general for your audience and that a more direct experience is required. Whatever the reasoning, make the writing more meaningful for the readers.

As you write more and more, you will begin to come up with revision questions that relate directly to your strengths and weaknesses. Revision questions will help you remain focused and productive.

Is my essay well-organized? Am I on the right track?

By studying the framework of your essay, you may see where you need to improve. For instance, if you developed a narrative outline before writing your essay, make sure you have stuck to it. If you find that your essay is not sufficiently compelling, you may have to go back and revise the outline itself. If you didn't develop a narrative outline, work backward and create one from the essay. It should at least have a clear introduction, examples to support your thesis, and a compelling conclusion.

Are the details varied and sufficient?

Reread your supporting paragraphs closely. They should represent your strongest material. Try to recall if you have had any personal experiences (you can also relate those of others) that might illustrate your point better, or if there is any additional research you could do to make your point stronger. This part is especially important, because if your argument is weak, the essay fails. A good question to ask yourself is, "Is this thorough?" If it's not, you have more work to do.

Have you supported yourself?

Avoid the tendency to overgeneralize—that is, to make too many statements about broad groups of people such as men, women, Southerners, Democrats, or even teenagers. If you do make a generalization, make sure you explain your thinking behind it. If you say that, "People don't realize how tough it is being a teenager," you then have an obligation to explain just how tough it is being a teenager and why people don't realize it.

Is the writing "tight"?

Review sentences for overuse of "being" verbs, and replace them with "action" verbs. For instance, replace "She was going" with "She went." Use passive voice only when it's necessary. Check for key words that are repeated excessively throughout the essay and find clear, appropriate synonyms to take their place. Rewrite any sentences that seem awkward.

DON'T BE PREDICTABLE

Clichés are a sign of lazy writing. Eliminate them and your writing will improve. If you wrote, "He spoke a mile a minute," rewrite it with a plain but creative phrase such as "He spoke with the speed of an auctioneer in a hurry."

Are parts of the essay too complicated?

Remember your audience. Your readers may be less knowledgeable than you about the topic. If an explanatory section is too verbose or complex, delete it and start again. If you're having trouble here, consider how you'd explain something to a fourth-grader. Perhaps instead of saying "The mechanism features interlocking metal parts that bond to form an air-tight seal," you could say, "The device works like a zipper." This doesn't mean being oversimplistic, it just means explaining things in simple terms. They're not the same thing.

Are parts of the essay too simple?

Sometimes, you might be so convinced that a statement is valid that you feel you don't need to explain it much. It's as though this chapter were composed of one line of advice: "Make sure your essay is interesting," and leaving it at that. Even though the statement is true and makes sense, a closer look reveals that you should have more to say.

EDITING FOR SUBJECT

One of the major issues you will address as your own editor (or as a peer editor) is that of subject. As you read, ask these questions:

Is this subject interesting?

What's interesting to one reader may not be interesting to another. All you can do is make sure you find the subject interesting and that you effectively express that enthusiasm. Your audience does not necessarily need to have an interest in your subject—but it does need a reason to care about your topic. In politics, if an essay sought to explain why your own party's views are out of step with Americans' beliefs, you might be interested enough to give it a read.

In the same way, personal essays can be interesting because they often reflect the development of a person's identity. An author may write about how her involvement in an obscure yoga program helped her take control of her life. Many readers may not care about the yoga, but they'll read anyway because they're interested in the idea of a person taking control of her life.

Is this subject significant?

Significant, in this instance, does not necessarily mean the subject must be of grave concern. It does mean that the subject should be relevant to the readers—that in some way, they will benefit by reading your work. If your essay is intended to inform, you should have reason to believe that your audience will appreciate being informed. Likewise, if your essay is intended to entertain, it should bring a smile to their faces.

Does the writing sustain reader interest?

If you're like most writers, you probably put a great deal of thought into your introduction, knowing that if you bore your readers within the first few lines, they won't read on. It's equally important to remember that readers will put down your work if it doesn't sustain a level of quality. Be sure the information in your supporting paragraphs further engages readers and piques their curiosity. They should want to know more with each paragraph. Finally, your conclusion should reflect the points you've made and leave readers thinking about your subject.

A "no" answer to any of these questions means the writing may not be effective and requires revision.

Read the following text, and think about the questions above.

Magazines: A Smart (-Alecky) Read

Ah, college. Where else but in lectures and late-night bull sessions could you spend hours pondering the mysteries of the universe, the wonders of civilization, the truth about Pop Rocks and soda? Well, there's *Mental Floss*. The year-old magazine is a lot like that professor of yours who peppered his tests with raunchy jokes: it makes learning fun. The current issue, for instance, reveals that "unlike people," stars get hotter as they age. Oh, and Pop Rocks and soda won't kill you.

The Original Five *Mental Floss* staffers had no journalistic experience, except for one kid who'd worked on his high-school newspaper. Now they run a bimonthly with 10,000 subscribers and a newsstand presence of 50,000 copies. Sixty percent of those get sold, an almost unheard-of statistic for new magazines. Recently the staff has inked deals for a book series, a board game, radio spots and a syndicated column. "We haven't spent a dime on marketing," says cofounder Will Pearson. "We still don't know why it's worked so well." Maybe it has something to do with the magazine's breezy, *Maxim*-style blurbs, or its advisory board, stocked with influential journalists who have spread the word. Or it could be the gimmicks, like that title ("God, we thought of some awful names at first," says Pearson) or the tag line: "Feel smart again." Either way, it's clear the *Mental Floss* folks have been reading their own magazine.

—Mary Carmichael, *Newsweek*, December 23, 2002

Now answer the following questions:

Is the subject interesting?

Yes. It's interesting because it's about something fun—and it is written in an enthusiastic manner. The article mimics the appeal of *Mental Floss* itself by making reference to Pop Rocks, soda, and raunchy jokes. It goes on to tell of an improbable success story—and that is very appealing.

Is the subject significant?

Yes. The article connects with people who have been to college, as well as people who read magazines. *Newsweek*, which appeals to college-educated readers, is a perfect fit! Though this story has no urgency, it is highly informative and entertaining. It tells readers about a new product (maybe they'll even subscribe), and it amuses us as well.

Does the writing sustain reader interest?

Though this is a short article, the writer sustains our interest with her relaxed, conversational tone (e.g., "Ah, college" or "Oh, and Pop Rocks and soda won't kill you"). After reading the first few lines, we want to know what *Mental Floss* is. After reading the start of the second paragraph, we also want to know how these guys became successful. The article raises and answers questions. By doing so, our interest is sustained.

EDITING FOR AUDIENCE

Some writers do not understand who their readers are. They write to impress by using complex vocabulary and long, involved sentences that result in unclear messages. In the end, they neither impress nor communicate.

Before beginning to write, think about who will be reading your essay. You want to produce writing that's easy to understand and enjoyable to read.

Evaluate your writing using these "Audience Awareness Guidelines":

Choose simple words rather than complicated words.
Do write: I'd like you to stop playing the music so loud.
Don't write: I'd appreciate the cessation of loud music.

Use active voice rather than passive voice whenever possible.

Do write: The running back carried the football.

Don't write: The football was carried by the running back.

Use specific, precise words.

Do write: Karen drove to Chicago.

Don't write: Karen went to Chicago.

Eliminate needless words.

Do write: I won't attend the party because I'm working that night.

Don't write: I won't attend the party for the reason that I'm working that night.

Link ideas and paragraphs with transitions.

Do write: I love Italian food, though I don't like calamari or pesto.

Don't write: I love Italian food. I don't like calamari. I don't like pesto.

Keep the sentences short—they're easier to read.

Do write: The Democrats favored tax cuts as a way to win favor with voters who want government policies favorable to their economic situations. As voters, they are concerned with their standard of life.

Don't write: The Democrats were the proponents of tax cuts, because they saw this as a way to win favor with the voters who were looking for government policies that favored their economic situations, as voters should be because the standard of life is a major concern to them.

EDITING FOR PURPOSE

A clear sense of purpose is a key standard in determining whether a piece of writing is effective or ineffective. After all, if you don't have an identifiable goal with respect to your writing, you'll have a harder time organizing ideas and choosing words. That's something that is bound to affect the reader.

When you're trying to persuade the reader of something, make sure that is expressed in the introduction. You might use wording such as, "These examples show . . .," "I have discovered . . .," or "The evidence demonstrates that . . ." to make sure your position is clear. Follow-up paragraphs should contain examples and details, avoiding overuse of "I believe . . ." The supporting evidence should encourage the reader to independently draw the same conclusions you have stated at the beginning.

When you're writing to inform or educate, the emphasis is on facts and the tone is objective. Whether you're explaining the Electoral College or documenting the history of the computer industry, your writing should steer clear of opinion and perception. Supporting points should document the issue at hand. Make sure your writing doesn't guide your reader to a way of thinking. If it does, your words need editing.

When you're writing to entertain, the rules are more relaxed. The overriding concern is to *stick to the point*. Don't let being original or funny get in the way of your message. It helps to have a central theme that you return to, even if the story is about getting your driver's license. Check to see that your entertaining story is told in chronological order, or at least has some logical organization. Just because it's creative doesn't mean it can be all over the place.

PROOFREADING

Proofreading is the final step in the entire process. This is the time when you look for stray errors in spelling, grammar, or style. You might find a misplaced punctuation mark or a misspelled word: Perhaps *an* was supposed to be *and.*

Proofreading is absolutely essential. A story may be brilliantly told, constructed, drafted, and written, but if it's full of annoying errors, the reader will become insulted at the lack of care invested (and probably confused by many of the mistakes—is that word *collected* or *corrected*?).

USE A SPELLING CHECKER WITH CAUTION

Much has been written about how spell-checking programs won't catch all errors. There is some truth to that, but the programs do catch many mistakes that befall writers. Just don't automatically click "change" for every suggestion it makes, since it might be wrong.

Both editing and proofreading require at least three things: time, a brightly colored pen (though not red—see more on this in chapter 15), a dictionary and style book (or grammar book with editing marks). Editing and proofreading work best on a hard-copy printout; on a computer screen, it's all too easy to overlook mistakes. Therefore, print out your writings before you edit and proof them.

EDITING CHECKLIST

Use this checklist to help you revise your work. Make notes as you work through the checklist.

INTRODUCTION

    A. Does your lead-in sentence generate interest?

    B. Is your theme statement clear and well placed?

    C. Are details directly relevant to the theme? Do they suggest what will come?

SUPPORTING PARAGRAPHS

    A. Do you have transitions between paragraphs?

    B. Is the topic sentence clear and well placed?

    C. Are details specific, interesting, and related to the topic sentence and theme?

CONCLUSION

    A. Do you repeat or refer to your theme statement?

    B. Are your important points briefly summarized?

    C. Do you have any statement of meaning or conclusion about the importance of your experience or theme idea?

LANGUAGE

    A. Are sentences correctly connected and verbal phrases accurately placed?

    B. Do sentences begin with their subjects? Are your verbs active?

    C. Do sentences say what you want them to; are they clear?

SPELLING AND GRAMMAR

    A. Check for spelling and grammar mistakes and correct them.

Select either an essay of yours or an article of your choice that discusses a subject of interest to you. After carefully reading it, answer these questions:

1. Did you or the writer appear to understand the audience?

2. How does the article begin? Does the writing show an understanding of the audience?

3. What type of reader might be confused by the essay? What specifically might be confusing or unclear?

CHAPTER TEN

Rules of Attribution

The word *attribution* comes from the word *tribute*, which in ancient times referred to a payment from one ruler or nation to another in exchange for protection. In current usage, a *tribute* is an acknowledgment or something given as due and deserved. Surely you have heard of something done as "a tribute to one's dedication and hard work."

In writing, it is necessary to give credit to the sources for your ideas. Attribution does just that. Rules of attribution are the systematic way that writers recognize the sources for their ideas.

It is common in writing to draw on the ideas of others. When you do this, you are required to credit those ideas to the original authors. If you don't, you are plagiarizing. Whether or not you use exact words from another text, you must give credit where credit is due. In other words, you're telling the reader that these ideas were built up from those of another author or text.

The key rules of attribution are:

- If you are using the exact words of a source, you must either enclose them in quotation marks or use the "long quotation form."

- You must give credit to the ideas of a source whether you quote those ideas directly or rephrase them.
- You must give credit within the paragraph where you mention ideas from an outside source, and in formal academic work, at the end of your paper in a Works Cited page.

WHAT TO ASK

In order to determine whether attributions are appropriate for your essay, ask yourself the following basic questions:

Whose words are you using?

If you are taking a direct quote, you must set the exact wording within quotation marks. If it's a long quote, indent it in the middle of the page, and since it is set off, quotes are not necessary. You must identify the author in parentheses and the text from which the quote was taken.

Whose idea is it?

Similarly, you must give credit to the source of an idea. This specifically includes when you paraphrase—put something into your own words—or summarize an idea. On the other hand, ideas that are common knowledge and are mentioned by a source do not have to be credited to that source.

HOW TO GIVE CREDIT

The following paragraph is taken from the fictitious article "Our Dependence," by Fred Williams.

> If everyone were to stop driving SUVs we wouldn't need as much oil. Our dependence on foreign countries would be reduced and we might not spend so much of our time planning to go to war with states that have the resources that we want.

There are three options for crediting this information:

Method #1: For a direct quotation that is three or fewer lines of typed text, keep it within the body of the text but put quotation marks around the quote. Then, put the author's name in parentheses after the quotation.

> One writer has an interesting theory: "If everyone were to stop driving SUVs, we wouldn't need as much oil" (Williams, 21).

Following the quotation in parentheses is the author's name and the page number on which it was found. This information should also be referenced in more detail in a Works Cited page at the end of your paper.

Method #2: For long quotations (longer than three lines of typed text), do not put quotation marks around the quote; rather, indent the entire text in the middle of the page and follow directly with the author's name in parentheses.

> One writer has an interesting theory:
>
> If everyone were to stop driving SUVs we wouldn't need as much oil. Our dependence on foreign countries would be reduced and we might not spend so much of our time planning to go to war with states that have the resources that we want (Williams, 21).

Assuming that this text was more than three lines long, it would be indented; this replaces the quotation marks. Following the quotation in parentheses is the author's name and the page number of the source, which you will include in more detail in a Works Cited page at the end of your paper.

Method #3: For a paraphrased idea, you do not use the exact words of the source. When you just summarize an idea, put the author's name in parentheses after you have summarized the idea. No quotation marks are necessary, and the text does not have to be indented.

One author believes that Americans should abandon Sport Utility Vehicles. By doing this, our country could become more independent. This could keep us from having conflicts with nations that have the oil we now need (Williams, 21).

The student here has replaced key words from the original text with words of his own. *Everyone* was replaced by *Americans*; *stop driving* by *abandon*; *war* by *conflicts*; and *states* by *nations*. Also, the wording has changed so that now, quotation marks would not be appropriate. The phrase *Our dependence on foreign countries would be reduced* was changed to *our country could become more independent.*

Though the wording here has been paraphrased, credit must still be given to Williams for his idea. Place the author's name and page number in parentheses following the paragraph.

AN EXAMPLE

Following is how three students considered incorporating information taken from another source. That source, a *Newsweek* article called "Al Qaeda: Alive and Killing," refers to a tape purportedly made by Osama bin Laden, and to the Bush administration's concerns about whether the tape was real.

> ### IDEAS MUST BE CREDITED, TOO
> Even if the words and the word order you use are your own, the original author must be given credit for the idea!

First, let's look at some of the original text:

At last, it seemed, they knew. For nearly a year, the question loomed: had bin Laden been killed in the devastating U.S. bombing campaign, or had he somehow managed to escape and lie low, possibly in the lawless border region between Afghanistan and Pakistan? Some audio experts said the sound quality on the tape was too poor for a 100 percent match. But technical analysts at the secretive National Security Agency believe it would have been almost impossible for even the most skilled Qaeda hoaxter to convincingly cut and paste the message together from bits of old bin Laden speeches and broadcasts (Hosenball, Isikoff, and Lipper, *Newsweek*, November 23, 2002).

Now let's examine how the three students tried to use this information. After reading each example, jot down whether you believe the example is acceptable or plagiarized (does not correctly apply rules of attribution). If you believe that the item is plagiarized, explain why. Refer specifically to the original quotation as you make your decision.

Example One:

Osama bin Laden's Al Qaeda network of terrorism had been responsible for the September 11th attacks on the United States. The administration had been worried about Osama bin Laden and at last they knew. For nearly a year, the question loomed: had bin Laden been killed in the devastating U.S. bombing campaign, or had he somehow managed to escape? Technical analysts at the National Security Agency believed the tape was not a hoax (Hosenball and others).

Acceptable or Plagiarized? Explain.

Example Two:

The administration wanted to know if the bin Laden tape was a fake. However, the secretive National Security Agency's technical analysts believed that it would have been almost impossible for this tape to be faked.

Acceptable or Plagiarized? Explain.

Example Three:

> The administration was worried about the tape and now they had the answer. "... technical analysts at the secretive National Security Agency believe it would have been almost impossible for even the most skilled Qaeda hoaxter to convincingly cut and paste the message together from bits of old bin Laden speeches and broadcasts." (Hosenball and others) The sound quality on the tape was too poor for a 100 percent match.

Acceptable or Plagiarized? Explain.

All three examples are plagiarized: They did not properly give credit to the source. In each case, students used exact words of the source without quoting. To verify this for yourself, go back to each example and circle the words that appear exactly as they did in the original source. Also take note of the fact that many "strings" of words appear next to each other.

In example one, the first sentence discusses Osama bin Laden; since that information is common knowledge, it does not have to be attributed. Yet you'll see that all the words after that are lifted right from the original source—and that requires quotation marks.

Similarly, in example two, sentence two, from *However* through *impossible*, the student copied the idea from the original without crediting the authors.

Example three appears to be fine at first glance. The student has quoted three lines (using the correct form) and given credit to the authors. But since the last line is also a direct quote, it must be credited to the author.

So just how should the students have incorporated the original article into their own essays? By paraphrasing; that is, by rewording it without any direct quotes. Also, the author of the original article should be given proper credit with an in-text citation.

The Right Way:

> So after year of wondering, the world now knows the truth. Bin Laden is alive. Members of the technical staff at the National Security Agency determined that the message from Osama bin Laden was genuine. They did not feel that Al Qaeda operatives had the technical skills to deceive the world by recording and combining parts of previously published bin Laden material (Hosenball and others).

HOW TO SUMMARIZE INFORMATION FROM A SOURCE

Review the following news brief and then write a summarizing paragraph. Incorporate most of the content in your own words, crediting the source as necessary. A good paraphrasing strategy is to read the original, then cover it up. Jot down what you think it meant. Then compare the two versions, keeping in mind the need for proper attribution.

North Korea: Diplomacy Hits the Wall

For the Bush administration, the worsening nuclear crisis in North Korea is turning into an exercise in frustration. For years conservatives inside the administration have longed to face down the Stalinist state. But now that they have a cast-iron case—satellite pictures show the North is moving its stockpile of nuclear fuel rods—they can only shrug their shoulders.

When North Korea took its first aggressive steps—by kicking out U.N. nuclear inspectors in December—the Bush administration decided to play it cool. They ruled out military strikes against the nuclear complex at Yongbyon, and instead of rushing to the United Nations for action, allowed the inspectors themselves to take the lead. Now that go-slow approach is going even slower than the Bush administration wants. After a month of diplomacy, the United States has hit a brick wall. American officials tell *Newsweek* that the Russian, Chinese and South Korean governments have effectively

---

blocked the nuclear inspectors from taking North Korea to the U.N. Security Council, where the United States had hoped to bring the world together against North Korea.

A board meeting of the United Nations' nuclear inspection group, the International Atomic Energy Agency (IAEA), was scheduled for this week. But South Korean officials requested yet another delay to allow for more diplomacy. The reality has been American exasperation while North Korea stages ever more aggressive moves. "We can't get the Russians and the Chinese to help us get the IAEA to live up to its mandate," said one senior administration official. U.S. officials say the Chinese government is deeply split over the issue, annoyed by the North Koreans but also fearful that the regime will collapse on its doorstep. The Russians, for their part, are suffering "bureaucratic inertia," according to the administration. In the meantime, the North Koreans are exploiting the crisis in Iraq to place added pressure on Washington. U.S. officials are waiting for the North to stage its next aggressive step in an attempt to shock Washington into agreeing to a big new aid package. "I anticipate a missile test probably five to eight days after we launch military strikes against Iraq," says one administration official. Where North Korea is moving its fuel rods, nobody really knows. What U.S. officials do know is that the fuel rods—which were kept under seal since 1994—can be rapidly reprocessed into weapons-grade plutonium. North Korea, which already sells missiles to anyone who can pay hard cash, could soon go into full-scale production of nuclear weapons. That prospect—which once filled conservatives with horror—is now met with a giant question mark. "If a country is hellbent on developing nuclear weapons," says one official, "what can you do?"

—Richard Wolffe, *Newsweek*, February 10, 2003

Now, examine your summary more closely. Circle any words you used from the original. Other than specific names of countries or places, did you use the exact words anywhere? Do you have long strings of word-for-word quotes? If so, did you put them in quotation marks? In paraphrasing, did you change the sentence structure (word order) from the original? Did you give credit to the source itself?

CREDIT THE SOURCES

To complete the process of attribution, you should add a final section or page that cites all the sources you used in your writing. Sample citations below correspond to the Modern Language Association— or MLA—style, though your instructor may suggest an alternative. Carefully review all the punctuation in each citation. Also note that citations are formatted in "hanging paragraphs," with first lines starting at the left margin and all succeeding lines indented.

For a book (single author):

Author's last name, author's first name. *Title of Book*. City published: Publisher, year.

- Ambrose, Stephen. *Undaunted Courage*. New York: Simon & Schuster, 1996.

For a book (multiple authors):

- Cooper, William, et al. *The American South*. New York: McGraw Hill, Inc., 1991.

For a signed magazine article or essay:

Author's last name, author's first name. "Article Title." *Magazine Title* Date: page.

- Alter, Jonathan. "At the Core of Nuclear Fear." *Newsweek* 24 June 2002: 40.

For an unsigned magazine article or essay:

"Article Title." *Magazine Title* Date: page.

- "The Uprising." *Headhunter Magazine* 23 April 1947: 58.

For a newspaper article:

"Article title." *Newspaper Title* Date: Page.

- "Consumer Group Issues Toy Safety Warning." *Morning Sun*
  27 November 2002: 37.

For a source from the Internet:

Your goal here is to direct the reader to the specific Web page. If the page contains an author or article, place those first, but you need to include the specific Web address. You can copy and paste this address from your browser locator or else you can retype it. The following source refers to an unsigned *Newsweek* article on line.

- "N. Korea Bans Use of U.S. Dollars." www.msnbc.com
  23 November 2002.
  <http://stacks.msnbc.com/news/839031.asp>

Sample "Works Cited" Page

(Note that all references are in alphabetical order.)

Alter, Jonathan. "At the Core of Nuclear Fear." *Newsweek*
24 June 2002: 40.

Ambrose, Stephen. *Undaunted Courage.* New York:
Simon & Schuster, 1996.

"Consumer Group Issues Toy Safety Warning." *Morning Sun*
27 November 2002.

Cooper, William, et al. *The American South.* New York:
McGraw Hill, Inc., 1991.

"N. Korea bans use of U.S. dollars." msnbc.com
23 November 2002. <http://stacks.msnbc.com/news/839031.asp>.

"The Uprising." *Headhunter Magazine* 23 April 1947: 58.

Section II

TYPES OF WRITING

CHAPTER ELEVEN

Writing for Standardized Tests

Standardized tests such as the ACT and SAT require you to use a form of writing known as *persuasion*. This chapter will first discuss the basics of persuasive writing, and then apply those tenets to the requirements of the SAT and ACT tests.

WHAT APPROACH TO TAKE WITH YOUR ESSAY

The art of persuasion is something we learn from an early age. Our earliest attempts at language involve trying to convince others—often our parents—to do what we want and to convince them of our position. Often, we are successful, such as the two-year-old who repeats the word *cookie* until rewarded, or the young driver who persistently asks for the car keys.

In the same way, our effectiveness as we get older has a great deal to do with our language skills; that is, how well our reasoning holds up to our requests.

The Persuasive Angle

Persuasive writing is designed to make a reader think a certain way about an idea. The persuasive essay is at the core of educational discourse and follows a basic format: introduction, body, and conclusion. The introduction clearly states the writer's opinion or *thesis*, which is the main idea of the essay. The essential ingredient is proving this point to your reader.

> ### LANGUAGE IS POWER
>
> Language is a tool that people and governments use to attain their objectives. Effective persuasion literally shapes the world.

Persuasive writing is, in effect, a good argument. And a good argument must go beyond the bounds of just contradiction. Think of the most simplistic form of verbal sparring: "Yes it is!" "No, it isn't!" "Yes it is!" It's unconvincing, to say the least. A sound argument must be supported with more than just emotion—it must be based on examples and references to specific facts. The first step to doing this is to clarify your position on the issue. Don't assume that your reader knows what that is. What precise opinion do you support?

The key elements of a persuasive essay are:

- A clearly defined position in a logical thesis sentence
- Sound supporting examples with unbiased facts
- Discussion of arguments on the opposing side of the issue

Present a Clearly Defined Position

The first thing you must do in a persuasive essay is to present your point of view. Your thesis statement should be a definitive position about something. And while it should naturally be something you support (even if it's just for the length of the essay), it shouldn't be purely personal. In other words, aside from the fact that you believe in this position, it should be defendable by research and facts. Your opinion alone is not sufficient demonstration that this is a viable argument.

As you surely know from your personal life, persuasion often involves some emotion. As such, you may be tempted to appeal to your reader's emotion in your attempt to sway his view. Don't go this route in your essay. Your position will be significantly weakened if you play on sentimentality or empathy. The audience shouldn't have to feel bad or angry or sorry for something in order to be able to agree with it in principle.

Most SAT and ACT prompts (assignments) will involve a topic that can be argued on either side. Your thesis must present one side of an arguable point that is not "obviously true." That the American Revolution began in 1776 is not an arguable fact, and therefore insufficient as a persuasive topic or thesis.

Look at the thesis statement below. It states a clear opinion about an arguable fact. It's arguable because there's clearly another side: Some people may believe that flexibility—flex time, for example—only encourages workers to be lazy and to take advantage of the situation. However, your stating a side clearly is the key to your persuasive essay!

Statement: The more flexibility that workers are given in their jobs, the harder they will work.

Include Unbiased Facts

In order to effectively persuade, you must appear to be objective and unbiased. You must provide evidence along with some background information on the given topic. Each point should be developed one at a time; do not lump all your points together. Ideally, each paragraph should include no more than one, maybe two, points. More than that can confuse the reader.

Distinguish Between Opinions and Facts

Since your purpose is to persuade readers to think a certain way, your essay's *main idea* will naturally be a personal opinion. But the supporting reasons that you present to support this opinion should be facts—relevant, authoritative, and complete.

A good persuasive essay involves a thorough explanation of precisely why this position is "accurate." It includes both compelling reasons and facts. Stick to one or two key supporting facts per paragraph. You want to keep your argument streamlined and clear so that your reader will have an easy time processing the information.

Present the Opposing Side

Though you might be tempted to do so, do not entirely dismiss the "other side." After all, you can't effectively make your case if you don't first acknowledge that there's more than one way to look at the issue. You don't have to go into detail, but do mention that it exists in the broader context of the topic.

PICK THE SIDE THAT'S EASIER TO PROVE

For most class assignments, it won't matter which side of the argument you pick. From your perspective, choose the more convincing side and gather up all the supporting evidence.

A Model of the Persuasive Essay

Following is a good example of a persuasive essay. It states a compelling thesis: that insurance companies should not have access to private details about subscribers.

When Confidentiality is Compromised

People tell me their secrets. As a psychotherapist, I spend my days listening to men and women talk about their failures, their disappointments, their shame. They are often survivors of sexual abuse; some have been literally tortured by a parent or relative. Others have caused great injury to someone they love because of their own pain. All are wounded. Together we try to create a place of safety where frightening emotions can be discussed. But how can we do that when it is also my job to tell managed care companies about certain aspects of those discussions?

If a client wishes to have his therapy covered after an initial number of sessions, I am required to fill out a form requesting authorization for treatment. I have to answer a list of questions: Does the patient vomit after eating, steal, hallucinate, abuse drugs or alcohol? Does the patient want to kill himself or somebody else? Then I send the document off to the insurance company, where somebody who has never met my client decides if he's eligible to continue treatment.

Some of my clients are so uncomfortable with this arrangement they elect not to use their insurance at all. They have reason to be concerned. Where this most sensitive information ultimately ends up is always uncertain. Horror stories abound. Last year the Los Angeles Times ran a story describing how detailed psychological records of 62 patients were accidentally posted on the Web. That same year, a large drug company mistakenly disclosed the names of 600 psychiatric patients in a mass e-mail, and one of the country's biggest HMOs sent e-mails with confidential medical information to the wrong subscribers.

Therapy can be a harrowing experience. It is humbling and frightening, as the client struggles with old grief or shame. Often, clients come from families in which they never felt safe, where they did their best to hide or to escape from intrusive and abusive parents. Yet sometimes a client will find the courage to make himself vulnerable, to revisit a trauma he turned away from decades earlier.

The following scenario is based on several clients: I was sitting with a man who had been in therapy with me for more than a year. Fifty-five years old and sober the last 20. A good man, with a deeply troubled history and an intractable depression. He loved his family very much, but he could not believe that he deserved love in return. His greatest wish was to be dead. One day he walked into my office, sat down and closed his eyes. He took a deep breath and then looked up at the ceiling. He told me that one summer when he was 14 he had been sexual with an older neighborhood boy, whom he had admired. This boy had humiliated him in various ways, both physically and emotionally. My client had taken from this experience the belief that he was both utterly inadequate and unworthy as a human being.

His expectation, now that I knew about what had happened four decades earlier, was that I would reject him. I did not speak for a few seconds, struck by the pain in his voice and the shame on his face. I was reminded how great a privilege it is to be present when another person reveals himself. When I spoke I said something about the courage it must have taken to say what he had just said, and that I was moved. He took a breath. And then he said, his voice as small as a child's: "This isn't something you have to write down, is it?"

"No," I told him, feeling nonetheless complicit in this violation of his trust. Another insurance report was due in days, and although I would not reveal the specifics of our conversation, divulging anything at all about his symptoms and progress felt like a betrayal. There is no doubt that health-care costs are increasing rapidly, and insurance companies have a right to make a profit. But micromanaging their subscribers' psychotherapy is not the answer.

A better system is the one that's used by non–managed-care insurance companies. Instead of insisting that therapists disclose information about their clients, these companies simply make it clear that the subscriber is eligible for a certain number of sessions each year. This system is not perfect. There is always the chance that a seriously disturbed person will run out of benefits and be forced to pay out of pocket or, if his therapist is not willing to reduce the fee, stop treatment until the following year. Despite this problem, I still believe it's a better alternative to managed care, which undermines confidentiality—the very bedrock of effective therapy. I do not believe insurance companies need to know anything about the most private and painful aspects of our lives. If my clients are to heal, they must feel safe enough to speak the unspeakable.

—Trip Quillman, *Newsweek*, My Turn, May 6, 2002

USE PERSUASIVE WRITING ON STANDARDIZED TESTS

Writing is thinking! The ability to think critically is a key factor in being ready for college. Clear, well-organized writing is a way to demonstrate your critical thinking. It is your way to communicate that you have the skills to present your thoughts and ideas cogently and concisely. So it is important to prepare.

Preparation can involve the following:
- Being well-rested and ready to take the test
- Reflecting on aspects of your own life—your principles and values, your accomplishments, your friends, and those people who have influenced you
- Keeping in mind that you will have to respond to an assigned "prompt." Though none of the testing agencies expects you to think a certain way, they do expect you to think and write clearly.

SAT Essay

The SAT Writing Section includes a 25-minute essay prompt. This essay assignment is not optional, so you will have to complete it as part of the exam. You will be asked to develop a point of view on an issue, using logic and evidence based on reading, studies, experience, and observations. For instance:

Think carefully about the issue presented in the following excerpt and assignment below:

> If we want to be happy in life, we should not seek financial reward or fame for our achievements. Rather, we should seek personal satisfaction of a job well done as its own reward.
>
> **Assignment:** Are people motivated more by personal satisfaction or by money and fame? Plan and write an essay in which you develop your point of view on this issue. Support your position with reasoning and examples taken from your reading, studies, experience, or observations.

YOUR SAT ESSAY IS *NOT* EXPECTED TO BE PERFECT, BUT RATHER, A *CLEAN FIRST DRAFT*

A few minor errors are acceptable in your writing, so don't get caught up in making sure your essay is perfect.

With 25 minutes to write your essay, there is little time. Keep in mind that the test maker isn't expecting your essay to be perfect. Rather, it is looking for a solid first draft. A few minor errors are acceptable. At the same time, however, the criteria used to score your essay are rather strict, based on important writing skills.

Your answer sheet will include lines where you must write out your essay. You'll receive no other paper on which to write. There should be sufficient space as long as you write on every line, avoid wide margins, and keep your handwriting to a reasonable size.

ACT Writing Assessment

The Writing Test on the ACT is optional, though beginning in the fall of 2006, some postsecondary institutions will require it for admission. Check directly with the institution to which you will apply to see if it is required.

With a 30-minute deadline, you will respond to a prompt that defines an issue relevant to high school students. The prompt asks you to write about your perspective on the issue. The prompt will offer you a choice of two perspectives on the issue or you can define your own. For instance:

> Some people feel that dress codes are important for all schools because they improve the learning environment for students. Others believe that dress codes are too restrictive for students' individuality. In your opinion, should schools require dress codes?

> In your essay, take a position on this question. You may write about either one of the two points of view given, or you may present a different point of view on this question. Use specific reasons and examples to support your position.

Scoring of the SAT and ACT Essays

The most important thing to know with respect to scoring of your essay is this: *Write on the assigned topic.* An off-topic essay will get you a score of zero.

Evaluators will assign a grade based on how well you have understood the assignment, and on how well you have presented a logical defense of your perspective on the issue. Both the ACT and the SAT use a 6-point scale, with 6 being the best score and 1 being the worst (unless, of course, you get a 0 from having written off-topic).

Look at the scoring criteria for a perfect essay—a "6" essay. Whether writing for the SAT or ACT, the requirements are similar:

ACT Grading Criteria

For the top score of 6, your essay should:

- demonstrate that you have a clear understanding of the task
- present a clear position on the issue
- have an effective, well-developed introduction and conclusion
- be well organized with ideas presented in a logical order
- respond to complications of the issue, including counter-arguments
- explain your ideas fully and elaborately
- demonstrate a good command of language with varied sentence structure and precise word choice

SAT Grading Criteria

For a top score of 6, your essay should:

- effectively and insightfully develop a point of view
- demonstrate critical thinking
- reveal a logical progression of ideas
- use clear and appropriate reasons, examples, and other evidence
- exhibit a skillful use of language with varied sentence structure and appropriate word choice

PLAN FOR THE ESSAY BEFORE EVEN SEEING THE PROMPT

1. Examine your own beliefs: You should be able to link any writing prompt to experiences that have shaped your beliefs.

2. Consider any beliefs that differ from your own and think about why you don't support them. Some of those viewpoints will be useful in developing your supporting paragraphs–to show that your thoughts are well-balanced and have considered the "other side."

Plan Your Response Essay (5 minutes total)

The organizational steps that follow will help you produce a unified essay in a limited amount of time. Because of the critical time factor involved, make sure to cover all the key areas.

1. Take a stand

After reading the prompt, think about what position you will take. Go with your instincts or "gut feeling," about which side you can argue more effectively. Remember, though, that your *personal* opinion isn't relevant; what matters is what side you can make a better case for. With which position can you be more convincing?

Write down the stand you'll take in clear-cut language. It must be so clear that the reader will understand without question which side you are promoting. It is critical that your thesis directly responds to the prompt.

2. Make a list

List 4 ideas that you can use to support your position (don't write long sentences here—just fragments of ideas that will help you support your point). One of those ideas can be a counter-argument to a view opposite to your "stand," position, or thesis. Each of these elements could serve as the main idea of one of the paragraphs of the body of your essay.

3. Decide on the order of your ideas

Place your "strongest" idea first in the order, your second "strongest" last. These ideas should be supportable with facts and/or references to your own core beliefs and values.

Write Your Organized Response (15–20 minutes)

As you write, think of your life experiences and values—how can some of them be used in support of your reasons? Consider references to books or famous persons that might be used to support your stand on the issue.

1. Place your thesis or position on the issue as the first or second sentence of your introduction. Reread it a second and third time to make sure it responds to the prompt and clearly states your opinion on one side of the issue. This is critical to your success. Other sentences of your introduction can mention your key supporting ideas.

2. Write a brief paragraph for each supporting idea, developing your ideas. Include references to your own values, achievements, or creative works. You may also want to refer to your role models. Make certain that your reasons connect directly to your thesis. Also, in at least one of the paragraphs, make sure you refute an argument from the opposite side.

3. Employ good transitional devices to enumerate your reasons, using words such as *first, second, final,* or *in contrast.* Your essay should have a smooth flow from one paragraph to the next.

4. Finally, in your conclusion, summarize your point—restating your position. Vary the wording, however, so that it isn't simply a mere repetition of what has been said. Conclude with an effective ending that will convince the reader of your beliefs.

Review Your Response (5 minutes)

Many writers neglect to review their work. In fact, you should be the first person to *read* your response. Read it! Nothing is more important than that. Read it slowly and make changes where appropriate.

Check to see that your response:

- Has a clear position and you have articulated both sides of the issue, refuting at least one counter-argument
- Backs up your opinions with examples and facts, and that you have presented a substantiated point of view
- Acknowledges the other side of the issue and explains why it isn't as valid an opinion as yours
- Uses rich and varied wording. (If it doesn't, change some words and phrases that will enhance your breadth of language.)
- Concludes leaving the final impression you desire

PRACTICE RESPONDING TO TEST PROMPTS

Do not look at the prompts that follow until you are ready to spend a solid 30 minutes applying what you have learned. Write your responses on *paper*—not computer—to simulate actual test conditions.

Sample Prompt 1

Because of their "questionable" content, certain novels are banned from some schools' curriculum, with school governing boards citing "unsuitability" and "inappropriateness with respect to community standards for decency." Some of the banned novels, however, have won awards of excellence.

Some people argue that banning these novels from high school seniors is censorship, and that seniors ought to be able to read and discuss any work of literature in a classroom setting. Others support strict guidelines for allowable reading material, based on their interpretation of community standards.

In your opinion, should seniors in high school be restricted from reading certain works of literature? Your response should take a clear position on this issue, and you may write about either side. Use specific examples and reasons to defend your point of view.

Sample Prompt 2

"A friend is someone with whom I can be sincere." (Ralph Waldo Emerson)

Assignment: What is your view on the idea that a person should always be able to confide in a friend without fear? Support your position with reasoning and examples from your own reading, experiences, or observations.

FINAL REVIEW

Evaluate your response to one of the prompts to determine whether you have included all pertinent sections. Refer to the list in "Reviewing your Response" as given above.

CHAPTER TWELVE

Writing for College Applications

The college application essay is an essay with a twist. You want to present a compelling view of yourself and/or your ideas; you want your essay to help make you stand out. You're also trying to convince the college that you have something to contribute.

Whatever view you present, it is to your advantage to get background information on the institution to which you are applying. That way, you can put your thoughts in context, and your essay will come across as more honest and focused. The more you know about whom you are writing for, the more effective your essay will be. Beyond that, you are trying to demonstrate what you can do with your writing. How will your writing fare once you are in college-level classes?

WHAT COLLEGES LOOK FOR IN AN ESSAY

On the whole, colleges and universities look for students who indicate depth and maturity in their interests and thinking. They want to see personal honesty and logical focus, not vague generalities. They don't want you to give them what you think they want to hear—a listing of your achievements or a rehash of generalities like world peace.

Admissions readers want to know about you as a real person, not as an ideal candidate who is an abstraction. Are you intellectually curious? Are you artistically talented? Are you motivated to learn? Do you demonstrate initiative?

Schools want students who have some insight into their life experiences. They want to know how your responses have deepened your perspectives and changed your outlook and/or behavior. They also want to see evidence of your intellectual interests and breadth of knowledge. They're not interested in an essay discussing anything in vague general terms. Be specific in your choices and your language.

GO BEYOND LISTING BASIC FACTS

When writing your essay for college, you *must* get past objective facts and description. Your essay needs a unique angle. It will be the only chance on paper you'll get to reveal your personality.

THREE TYPES OF ESSAYS

College applications tend to ask for one of three types of essays: the **personal statement**, the **persuasive essay**, and the **offbeat essay**.

The Personal Statement

If the college provides a prompt for a personal statement (e.g., "What work of literature or art or science has challenged you, and in what way?"), it will be open-ended. The prompt that appears on the application form will guide you in determining which type of essay to write. The prompts below—used by real schools in the past— would require a *personal statement*.

- "How would you describe yourself as a human being? What quality do you like best in yourself and what do you like least? What quality would you most like to see flourish and which would you like to see wither?" (Bates College)

- "Creative people state that taking risks often promotes important discoveries in their lives or works. Discuss a risk that has led to a significant change (positive or negative) in your personal or intellectual life." (Simmons College)

In responding to this type of prompt, choose the challenge *most difficult* and *specific to you* personally. Narrow it down to a dramatic example—something that you feel conveys the sense of challenge you face—and write with vivid specific details. Your focus must be on what the challenge meant to you and how you handled it. Include your emotions and be direct and honest about the problems.

REFER BY NAME TO THE SCHOOL TO WHICH YOU ARE APPLYING.

Admissions readers want to feel that their school is where you would like to be. Explain why you're a perfect match.

One feature of the personal statement is the examination of *personal growth and self-understanding*. You must be honest—and vulnerable—about events in your life, and make an effort to arrive at some insight about them. No one is asking you to disclose confidential details, but you should reveal something important about yourself. Writing about how you overcame an obstacle or were shaped by a certain event may make you uncomfortable, but you need to get past it. Why? Those things reveal who you are, and colleges want to know students before they offer an admission letter.

While you don't want to sound arrogant, honest confidence about what you have learned or experienced will be perceived as a positive. This doesn't mean you should hesitate to express fears and anxieties. That's a normal part of life. Learning how to deal with those fears is what makes you unique. Be sure you also communicate what you learned (or did) as a result. Admissions officers aren't looking for perfect applicants; they are looking for how you approach the challenges that life throws you.

A Model of the Personal Statement

The following essay won the grand prize in the 2003 Kaplan/*Newsweek* My Turn Essay contest. It is also an excellent example of a personal statement. It reveals the author's personality, interests, breadth of knowledge, and depth of insight—not to mention an excellent writing ability.

How I Came to Rule the Lego Universe

By Paula Fortner

I built my childhood on Legos. Unlike most girls I know, I grew up with Star Trek, Space Invaders, and the Air and Space Museum. Although I owned dolls and dress-up clothes, to play with my brothers required a Lego base.

From the beginning, I realized I could never compete with the intricate aircraft of my older brother, Neil, the first-place winner in a Lego contest at age 6. I also learned not to provoke my younger brother, Glen, who stomped through our world like Godzilla, smashing his tiny fists into control towers and cockpits. Though I could not match Neil's technological superiority, or Glen's brute force, it did not take long for me to dominate them both. In the basement corner that became our universe, I first tasted the power of market economics and diplomacy.

For my first official action, I declared a currency. A flat, one-by-one Lego piece represented the basic monetary unit, called a Koka. My announcement sparked the Great Koka Rush of '94, during which we ransacked all three industrial-sized Lego bins. I made a decent Lego miner, but soon diverted my energy to the construction of simple products. I built cars, hovercraft and weapons, then hoarded control panels, wheels and antennae. Using these, I set up the first general store in our solar system. My brothers flocked to my store, eager to spend their newly acquired wealth. Of course I helped them out."

"Glen, I'd love to sell you this stealth car I made. Unfortunately, Neil has been talking about needing a spy craft too. He's offering 30

Kokas for it, but I really think you'll need some defense soon, from what he's planning. I want to sell it to you, but only if you can offer 35 Kokas. I can sell it to you for 30 if you're interested in purchasing this knight statue as well, only 10 additional Kokas. Just think of what it could do for the morale on your base!"

Those tiny yellow men and women of mine became very effective salespeople. Perhaps it was their constant, charming smiles.

Although everything usually ran smoothly in the galaxy, every few months my brothers prepared for war against each other (as brothers often do). I never remained neutral in these conflicts; I always took both sides. Knowing my base would soon receive defense contracts, I stocked up on airplane pieces and lasers before the battles really started. If Neil ran low on Kokas before a war, I commissioned him to build fighter planes using my stockpile. He collected payment in return, and I used the planes as merchandise in my store. If Glen realized he needed more fighters, I often sold him those that Neil originally crafted. This put Neil in the vexing position of being attacked by the weapons he invented. The analogy to today's world was not so apparent at the time.

The wars usually ended with smashed piles of colored bricks and lots of tears. This is when I did most of my charity work, offering rebuilding services and no-interest loans. I can trace my interest in diplomacy to the moments when I struggled to mend relations between two war-torn bases. My little Marshall Plan helped them to recover economically, and soon I got them on speaking terms, so we could resume free trade. Neil specialized in planes and cars, Glen specialized in control towers and buildings, and I ran the market. Production peaked during peacetime, but it was never long before they descended once again into war.

The 30-Days War that almost obliterated Neil's base marked the decline of the Lego Empire. Neil had become too old for Legos anyway, and never rebuilt his base. For a while Glen and I competed to fill the power vacuum but without alliances and simultaneous negotiation most of the fun was missing. Eventually, the bases were abandoned. Neil moved on to flying real planes and majoring in aerospace engineering. Glen progressed to K'nex and

> programmable robotics kits. As for myself, I've developed an
> interest in international relations on a less-miniature scale.
>
> Today our bases still stand, crumbling Parthenons that only hint
> at the glory that was our civilization. People who visit our house
> usually ask about the ruins and I tell them our history. I finish by
> showing them the Koka bins, one of the few things all three of us
> have intact. Neil and Glen barely had any money at the end, but my
> stash positively overflows. In a toy dominated by males, I held my
> own.
>
> —Paula Fortner, Kaplan/*Newsweek* "My Turn" Essay, 2003

Effective application essays combine certain elements. Those needed
for the personal statement are:

- Clarity of focus
- Logical development
- Depth of thought
- Personal growth
- Attention to writing

Clarity of Focus

Often, the most difficult thing about writing a personal statement is
finding the focus. The writer found hers in her experiences with her
Lego Universe. Hers is a tightly controlled essay that never loses its
focus on herself as ruler of that universe. In her opening paragraphs
she not only defines her theme, but states its importance: "In the
basement corner that became our universe, I first tasted the power of
market economics and diplomacy." This writer confidently knows
who she is and what she has learned from her experiences. That is
what admissions officers look for.

Logical Development

Fortner's subsequent paragraphs relate in specific details how she
developed her own dominance. Her use of her own dialogue is a

vivid way of illustrating her bargaining skills. Her careful selection of descriptive details allows her to insert humorous comments relative to both past and present. "...my brothers prepared for war against each other (as brothers often do). I never remained neutral in these conflicts; I always took both sides."

Depth of Thought

Fortner reveals her depth of insight and breadth of knowledge as she develops her essay. Her understanding of market economics becomes immediately apparent as she relates her actions. Her awareness of the relationship between the game and the world around us is revealed when she states: "This put Neil in the vexing position of being attacked by the weapons he invented. The analogy to today's world was not so apparent at the time." Her references to the Marshall Plan, the Parthenon, and—by analogy—the late Roman Empire reveal her knowledge of history as well as an understanding of their relationship to her childhood game.

Personal Growth

All of the ideas and examples detailed in the body of the essay reveal the growth of Fortner's understanding of how to take control of and profit, in some way, from the acts intrinsic to the game. As she does that, she relates her experiences to the larger world around her and reflects on what the game reveals about her own maturing interests: "I can trace my interest in diplomacy to the moments when I struggled to mend relations between two war-torn bases."

Attention to Writing

Fortner's writing skills are readily apparent. Her opening paragraphs catch the reader's interest, describe who and what she will be writing about, and introduce her theme. Her transitions between paragraphs are smooth: "Although everything usually ran smoothly in the galaxy...". Her specific details are vivid ("...who stomped through our world like Godzilla…"), move the reader through time (Neil at age 6 on to Neil in college), and are clearly related to her experience and theme.

The language of the essay flows easily from varied sentences to well-ordered paragraphs always appropriate to both subject matter and general audience. Fortner employs several figures of speech and an interesting metaphor linking the end of her Lego Universe with the late Roman Empire: "The 30-Days War…the decline of the Lego Empire." This leads into her conclusion in which she repeats her growing interest in international relations. Her final paragraph discusses the ending of her Lego universe and confidently asserts her own personal accomplishment: "In a toy dominated by males, I held my own."

The Persuasive Essay

Some application essay prompts ask for your opinion on an open-ended global issue for which there is no "right" answer. What the admissions readers look for in your responding essay is a focused, closely reasoned, persuasive argument. They don't care what your position is; they want to know how well you can present it.

The following college prompts call for a persuasive essay in response.

- "In your opinion, what is the greatest challenge that your generation will face? What ideas do you have for dealing with this issue?" (College of the Holy Cross)
- "Who do you feel has served as the strongest Afro-American role model in this [20th] century?" (Spelman College)

Good persuasion involves a thorough explanation of precisely what your position is and why it is "accurate." Your essay must include both facts and compelling reasons. You want to keep your argument streamlined and clear so your reader will have an easy time processing the information and being impressed with your presentation of it.

A persuasive essay goes beyond the bounds of simple contradiction. A sound argument must be supported with more than just emotion—it must be based on examples and references to specific facts. The first step to doing this is to clarify your position on the issue. Don't assume that your reader knows what that is.

As you know from your personal life, persuasion often involves emotion. You may be tempted to appeal to your readers' emotions in your attempt to sway their views. Don't go this route in your essay. Your position will be significantly weakened if you play on sentimentality or empathy in your discussion. You want your readers to perceive your own feelings, but they shouldn't have to feel bad or angry or sorry for something in order to be able to agree with it in principle.

A Model of the Persuasive Essay

In the following essay, a *Newsweek* columnist attempts to convince his readers of the negative effects of cell phones for himself and for our society. Whether you agree with him or not, he writes an engaging persuasive essay. (The *Newsweek* issues that followed had several Letters to the Editor responding to this essay.)

A Cell Phone? Never for Me.

Someday soon, I may be the last man in America without a cell phone. To those who see cell phones as progress, I say: they aggravate noise pollution and threaten our solitude. The central idea of cell phones is that you should be connected to almost everyone and everything at all times. The trouble is that cell phones assault your peace of mind no matter what you do. If you turn them off, why have **one**? You just irritate anyone who might call. If they're on and no one calls, you're irrelevant, unloved or both. If everyone calls, you're a basket case.

I'm a dropout and aim to stay that way. I admit this will be increasingly difficult, because cell phones are now passing a historic milestone. As with other triumphs of the mass market, they've reached a point when people forget what it was like before they existed. No one remembers life before cars, TVs, air conditioners, jets, credit cards, microwave ovens and ATM cards. So, too, now with cell phones. Anyone without one will soon be classified as a crank or member of the (deep) underclass.

Look at the numbers. In 1985 there were 340,213 cell-phone users. By year-end 2003 there were 159 million. (These figures come from the Cellular Telecommunications & Internet Association or CTIA.) I had once assumed that age, orneriness or hearing loss would immunize most of the over-60 population against cell phones. Wrong. Among those 60 to 69, cell phone ownership (60 percent) is almost as high as among 18- to 24-year-olds (66 percent), though lower than among 30- to 49-year-olds (76 percent), according to a recent survey from the Pew Research Center. Even among those 80 and older, ownership is 32 percent.

Of course, cell phones have productive uses. For those constantly on the road (salesmen, real-estate agents, repair technicians, some managers and reporters), they're a godsend. The same is true for critical workers (doctors, oil-rig firefighters) needed at a moment's notice. Otherwise, benefits seem murky.

They make driving more dangerous, though how much so is unclear. The Insurance Information Institute recently summarized some studies: the Harvard Center for Risk Analysis blamed cell phones for 6 percent of auto accidents each year, involving 2,600 deaths (but admitted that estimates are difficult); the AAA Foundation for Traffic Safety studied videotapes of 70 drivers and concluded that cell phones are distracting, though less so than many other activities (say, stretching for an item in the glove compartment).

Then, there's sheer nuisance. Private conversations have gone public. We've all been subjected to someone else's sales meeting, dinner reservation, family feud and dating problem. In 2003 cell phone conversations totaled 830 billion minutes, reckons CTIA.

That's about 75 times greater than in 1991 and almost 50 hours for every man, woman and child in America. How valuable is all this chitchat? The average conversation lasts two-and-a-half to three minutes. Surely many could be postponed or forgotten.

It's true that lots of people like to gab. Cell phones keep them company. Count that as a plus. But it's also true that lots of people dislike being bothered. These are folks who have cell phones but often wish they didn't. A recent poll, sponsored by the Lemelson–M.I.T. program, asked which invention people hated most but couldn't live without. Cell phones won, chosen by 30 percent of respondents.

Some benefits may be overstated. Cell phones for teens were sold as a way for parents to keep tabs on children. That works up to a point. The point is when your kids switch off the phones. Two of my teens have cell phones (that was Mom's idea; she has one too). Whenever I want them most, their phones are off. Hmm. Similar advantages are claimed for older people. They have cell phones to allow their children to monitor their health. This may spawn gallows humor on voice-mail messages. (For example: "Hi, Sonny. If you get this, I'm dead.)

Cell phones—and, indeed, all wireless devices—constitute another chapter in the ongoing breakdown between work and everything else. They pretend to increase your freedom while actually stealing it. People are supposed to be always capable of participating in the next meeting, responding to their emails or retrieving factoids from the Internet. People so devoted to staying interconnected are kept in a continual state of anxiety, because they may have missed some significant memo, rendezvous, bit of news or gossip. They may be more plugged in and less thoughtful.

All this is the wave of the future or, more precisely, the present. According to another survey, two thirds of Americans 16 to 29 would choose a cell phone over a traditional land line. Land lines have already dropped from 189.5 million in 1999 to 181.4 million at the end of 2003, says the Federal Communications Commission. Cell phones, an irresistible force, will soon pull ahead. But I vow to resist just as I've resisted ATM cards, laptops and digital cameras.

I agree increasingly with the late poet Ogden Nash, who wrote: "Progress might have been all right once, but it's gone on too long."

—Robert J. Samuelson, *Newsweek*, August 23, 2004
(c) 2004, *Newsweek*. Reprinted with permission.

The key elements of a persuasive essay are:

- Your own clearly defined position stated in a logical thesis
- Focused development of your view of the "prompt" issue
- Sound supporting examples with unbiased facts
- Discussion of arguments on the opposing side
- Attention to writing

Clearly Defined Position

The most important thing an admissions reader looks for in a persuasive essay is a logical statement of your position relative to the prompt question. This should be made obvious in your first paragraph, especially if you have been asked for your opinion on a specific matter. Your response must be personal and specific to you as well as to the prompt. If you are asked, for example, your opinion on the strongest Afro-American role model, identify the *who* and *why* right away. For the *why*, state your most important reason.

Samuelson's position on cell phones is clearly stated in a logical thesis in his first paragraph: "To those who see cell phones as progress, I say: they aggravate noise pollution and threaten our solitude." Note how specific he is; he does not say "To those who own cell phones." You know immediately that his focus is on the idea of cell phones as "progress." He has clearly and specifically defined the *what* and *why* of his personal argument.

Focused Development

It is easy to get off the track when you are writing an essay that must focus on your opinions as well as the prompt question. Keep your focus always on who or what you are writing about as well as your perspective on it. The main idea of each paragraph should refer back to your original thesis.

All of Samuelson's paragraphs refer to cell phones in one way or another. Even in a personal anecdote, he never loses a tight focus. "Two of my teens have cell phones (that was Mom's idea; she has one, too). Whenever I want them most, their phones are off. Hmm." These sentences personalize him by bringing in his family; they also utilize humor and interest, but they do not move into another subject.

Sound Supporting Examples

Without examples of the points you are trying to make, your essay will be just a bunch of generalities. Use the most specific factual examples you can find to give weight to your particular argument. Document your evidence: where and when did you read, hear or experience your examples. No college is going to be impressed by a "they say" presentation.

Most of Samuelson's essay contains specific factual examples for both sides of his argument. And he always gives the sources for his facts. It is one thing to throw out supportive numbers; it's another to state that they came from CTIA or the Pew Research Center, for example.

Discussion of Both Sides

In order to effectively persuade, you must be objective and unbiased. Though you might be tempted to do so, do not dismiss the "other side." Your reader will likely have a healthy skepticism in mind when reading your essay.

The opposing side ("Of course, cell phones have productive uses.") is presented early in Samuelson's essay. He then develops many of his paragraphs by providing pro/con examples. In fact, his personal argument is set against examples of the prolific uses of cell phones. He clearly wants the reader to know exactly why he disagrees with the majority "who see cell phones as progress."

Attention to Writing

Samuelson's essay is very carefully written. His first paragraph opens with an interest-catching sentence followed by his thesis. He uses clear transitions ("I'm a drop-out and aim to stay that way."), and his paragraph ideas never lose sight of his focus. His style is varied, personal and light. His final paragraph brings the reader back to his first paragraph: "But I vow to resist just as I've resisted ATM cards, laptops and digital cameras." And his final quote humorously repeats his point.

The Offbeat Essay

Some schools ask you to respond creatively to an aspect of your life or an unusual idea. The idea here is to assess your ability to see things from a different perspective—a unique angle that will reveal a great deal about you and your thinking.

The offbeat essay requires a rather sophisticated knowledge of how to use words to get your point across. Creative imagination is important not just in what you say, but in how you say it. If you cannot effectively present your perspective in your writing, that perspective will be lost.

The following prompts ask for an offbeat essay.

- "You have just completed your 300-page autobiography. Please submit page 217." (University of Pennsylvania)
- "For some prognosticators, the end of the world was in sight by the year 1000. How do you foresee your world of 2020?" (Dickinson College)

A Model of the Offbeat Essay

In "Fresh Fish," the essay model that follows, the author creatively reveals much about his background and weaknesses as well as his reflections about the growth he derived from this experience. (He focused very well on "page 217" of his biography.) He writes with clarity, simplicity, and emotion—bonus points for the humor. This essay was so effective the author used it in his application to Harvard University, which he now attends.

Fresh Fish

I can hear the snickers as I walk down the crowded sidewalks of Chinatown. The gossip at the vegetable stand. The grin of the fish man. The chatter from the seafood restaurants. Laughter is everywhere, like a dragon's tail winding throughout the streets.

I grew up speaking English, not Chinese, the language of my ancestors. The first word out of my mouth was *mommy*, not *mah mah*. When I was 3, my parents flashed cards with Chinese characters at my face, but I pushed them aside. My mom assured herself, "He will learn when he is ready." But the time never came. A decade later, I would regret that decision.

February 7, 1997, Chinese New Year: My relatives and I gather in my grandmother's three-room Mott Street apartment around the round kitchen table, half-hidden under boxes of *don tot, cha sui bao* and other Chinese delicacies from the local *dim sum* parlor. My Uncle Alex rapidly mutters something to me in Chinese, but all I can do is stare at him quizzically and scratch my head. "Still can't speak Chinese?" he teases me, now in English. "How old are you? 13? And you still can't talk to your grandmother, can't even buy a fish in Chinatown. What are you waiting for?"

"Hey, this is America, not China," I reply. "You want fish for dinner? I'll get some right now—with or without Chinese." I turn to my mom for permission, who reluctantly hands over a crisp $20 bill.

"Remember to ask for fresh fish, *sun seen yu*," she says. "You know how fussy your grandmother is with her fish." I repeat the words to my mother, who nods in approval, then dart down the two flights of dark, narrow stairs into the bright, crowded streets of Chinatown.

Following the foreign sounds and the smell of the ocean around the corner of Mott Street, I find the fish stand, submerged in a sea of customers. There are salmon and croaker and flounder and sea bass, fish with big eyes, fish with shiny scales, and fish that I've never seen before. "I'd like to buy some fresh fish," I blurt out to the fish man. But he ignores my English words and turns to serve the next customer. The cackling of the people behind me increases with their impatience. With every second, the breath of the dragons on my back intensifies—my blood boiling—compelling me to make my decision. What were my mother's words again?

"*Seen sang yu*, please," I stutter, jabbing at the sea bass. "Very *seen sang*," I repeat, this time, beaming at my simple eloquence. I had spoken Chinese, used it to communicate with my own people. I had... told a joke? The fish man suppresses a grin, but the crowd erupts with laughter and chuckles and snickers. They are Chinese; I am Chinese. I should feel right at home. Instead, I am the laughingstock, a disgrace to the language. My face turns red, like the color of *hung bao*, the red envelopes exchanged on Chinese New Year. Then, I am racing back to my grandmother's quiet apartment, the fish and the laughter in the distance.

I return to the apartment empty-handed, except for the now-wrinkled twenty-dollar bill that I clutch tightly in my pocket. "I asked for seen *sang yu*, fresh fish," I stammer when the door opens, "just like you told me to—I mean—didn't you tell me to say that? But ... but they just laughed."

For a moment, my mother simply grins to herself, saying nothing, holding me in suspense. Then she explains, "No, *sun seen* is fresh fish, not *seen sang*. You asked for a teacher fish. Even though fish travel in schools, you would have a really hard time trying to find the teacher."

My jaw drops. Should I laugh or cry? I still walk down Mott Street to visit my grandmother—past the fish man, past the vegetable stands, past the restaurant—concealing the fact that I cannot speak Chinese. Sometimes I laugh at my fish incident, but, in

> the end, the joke is on me. Every grin is a bond withering away; each chuckle, a culture lost; every giggle, my heritage fading away.
>
> —Christopher Chin, Honorable Mention, 2002 Kaplan/*Newsweek* "My Turn" Essay Competition

The important elements of offbeat application essays are:

- Your creative perspective on the prompt
- Clear focused development
- Depth of thought
- Personal growth
- Attention to writing

Creative Perspective

Though colleges using the offbeat prompt are looking for creativity and a unique perspective, they also want to see evidence of maturity. Don't get wildly creative. Admissions officers are looking for a perception that is unusual and capable of understanding, for example, that one well-told incident can convey significant personal meaning.

Chin's choice to write about a small event with ironic humor and a very specific focus results in a unique description of who he is and how he got that way. He also includes what he has learned from this experience. "Every grin is a bond withering away; each chuckle, a culture lost; every giggle, my heritage fading away." In a college application, statements like this are important.

Clear and Focused Development

In "Fresh Fish," the time frame is clear. The author's odyssey is chronicled vividly and in color—from apartment to fish stand and back to the apartment. Simple phrases such as "My relatives and I gather" and "I ... dart down the two flights of dark, narrow stairs" reveal the movement, and as readers, we're taken along. These phrases act as transitions that guide us through the passage of time.

While writing an essay in the first person present tense is not usually recommended, Chin gets away with it. The tight, logical flow of events—which presumably took place over the course of an hour—reflects a careful editing process. What he chose to leave out about that day is as important as what he chose to include.

Depth of Thought

The entire essay reveals Chin's depth of understanding that what seems, on the surface, to be an amusing incident has actually been an important experience that contributed much to his emotional awareness. "Sometimes I laugh at my fish incident, but, in the end, the joke is on me."

Personal Growth

Christopher Chin reveals his humiliation and shame. As readers, we can connect with these emotions because we all know them. "They are Chinese; I am Chinese. I should feel right at home. Instead, I am the laughingstock, a disgrace to the language. My face turns red, like the color of *hung bao*, the red envelopes exchanged on Chinese New Year."

Attention to Writing

Chin writes in clear, simple language that focuses on one personal event. His use of quotations is limited to precisely what he wants to convey. "'*Seen sang yu*, please,' I stutter, jabbing at the sea bass. 'Very *seen sang*,' I repeat, this time, beaming at my simple eloquence." These sentences tell readers exactly what he has asked for; they also reveal that he is unaware of his mistake and proud of what he has done. The irony involved in his emotions comes through without explanatory statements.

How does Chin share his emotion? He does so with humor—a humorous tale and a bittersweet tone. Deftly balancing the two perspectives of personal embarrassment with lighthearted humor, Chin poignantly illustrates an intimate event. We're allowed to laugh at the incident along with him. With a self-deprecating approach, he jokes about his decision to eschew the Chinese language.

While no doubt this is a reflective essay that reveals a sense of regret, the author has the presence of mind to realize that, from the perspective of an outsider, his story is amusing. He takes risks in his language, revealing his sorrow at how things transpired. Still, today, when he walks down the street in Chinatown, he hears "snickers" from those around him.

Chin's essay reveals the maturity of his knowledge of writing. He communicates his unique perspective with creativity, humor and a tight logical focus.

DEVELOPING YOUR ESSAY

Just as all the college essay prompts have a focus on you, the applicant, your college application essay will be a combination of the elements of the personal with the persuasive or offbeat essay. You must research yourself as well as your college. Reflect on events in your life that have helped shape who you are. Focus on your strengths, but—if necessary—provide a brief explanation of weaknesses you think important to inform your audience about.

DO SOME LEGWORK BEFORE YOU WRITE

Research in advance the types of prompts your chosen college has used, and practice writing response essays. This is particularly important if you are applying to a competitive university.

The first people at any college to read your essay are likely to be the newer staff in the Admissions Office. They want to be interested in what you say, not impressed by who or what you claim to know. Don't address your reader with, "To Whom it May Concern." It's evident who the reader is; there's no need to state it.

Your opening paragraph must grab reader interest and introduce your theme. Then, be sure each paragraph contains a topic sentence and the details relevant to it as well as the transitions connecting it. Paragraphs must be organized in a logical order that emphasizes the importance of what you want your readers to know about yourself and/or your convictions. If your essay deals with how you feel and/or what you think about some aspect of your life, you may want to choose an organization that describes that aspect and, then, present your reflections on it.

Don't Write a Biography

When you are asked to write about yourself—either specifically or in the context of a specific part of your experience—do not reply with a biography. Think about how your personality, knowledge, and interests mesh with what the school offers. How can these attributes be shaped to answer the specific question?

Start by making two lists: your personal attributes and your ideas. Then, choose what you consider the most important aspects of yourself as they relate to the college. Focus and organize that material and present it as creatively and succinctly as possible. You certainly don't want to just list your achievements in rote form; it's more about the style you present. Don't forget that admissions readers have thousands of essays to read in a year, so just listing a bunch of items won't do much to catch their eye.

The conclusion of a personal statement may be the most important part. The reader needs to walk away with the feeling that you are unique and that you are can make a difference—in your own life and in the lives of others. You will need, therefore, to emphasize the significance of what you have written.

Include Your Opinions

If the college prompt asks for a persuasive essay, write down several of your own points of view on the subject. Then, in order to clarify your own point of view, write the opposing side's position in a sentence or two.

When you plan your essay, anticipate what the opposing side would present and how best to address those points. You have to be able to articulate both sides of the issue before you begin writing. Once you have presented an opposing opinion, your job is to acknowledge that it is indeed valid but of small significance in the broader context of the topic. If you feel it isn't a valid argument at all, you should refute it in detail. Explain to readers why they shouldn't take stock in that opposing assertion.

Make sure your opinions are supported with facts and examples. Research the library or the Internet. You cannot present your point of view without validating it. Focus your essay on your view of the issue and be sure all your sentences have a specific relationship to it. Your conclusion should emphasize the final impression you want to convey. Clarify your viewpoint and leave the reader feeling persuaded.

Show Your Creativity

Be as creative as possible in promoting yourself and your perspective in response to the prompt. Brainstorm and jot down everything that comes to mind.

When you review what you've jotted down, consider which idea reflects the aspects of yourself that you want the college to know about. Is it an experience or perspective that can be developed in a creative, focused and logical manner? Will that development reveal your depth of thought, breadth of knowledge, and/or personal growth? You want to choose what will present you and your specific creative awareness in the best possible light.

Once you've made those choices, list all the relevant details you might use. Then, choose those that reveal the most about you and your perspective in a specific and vivid way. Organize those in a clear order of development that retains the focus of your essay. If you don't do this before you write your first draft, revise with it clearly in mind.

Writing generates thinking, so the first draft will likely call forth more ideas and details. The key is to focus and organize with each revision. Then review your language. Is your style appropriate to your subject and audience? Do sentences flow easily into paragraphs? Are your transitions between ideas smooth and clear? Can you make your details more specifically vivid? Can you use relevant similes and metaphors?

Finally, be sure your conclusion emphasizes what you want to tell the college about yourself. And don't forget to proofread.

CHAPTER THIRTEEN

Writing for Creative Purposes

Creative writing covers a wide area. This chapter discusses three types of creative essays: the descriptive, the personal, and the narrative. As one would expect, these essay types overlap.

The personal essay, for example, usually contains descriptive and narrative elements, but the focus is directly on the author. "The narrative is more about telling a meaningful *story*, often including effective description. However, the descriptive essay presents an impression—your impression—of something, with details that evoke the senses.

These kinds of writing styles are not mutually exclusive. Writing is an art, not a science, and you may blend elements as appropriate, depending on your subject and audience.

WHAT READERS LOOK FOR IN AN ESSAY

The first thing that readers look for in an essay is interest: Does the essay seem interesting? If your essay does not interest your reader, it won't be read. Few essays interest all readers, so a writer must know who he is writing for. Who will be reading it? When writing for your peers, your subject and style are sure to be different than if you're writing for an older, or more formal, audience.

The title and first paragraph may grab a reader, but the essay must sustain interest until its conclusion. Sustaining interest requires writing with clear focus and progression. Ideas should flow logically; language should be vivid with specific details. No matter how interesting a subject could be, vague generalities will not present it in a way that will hold reader interest.

The Descriptive Essay

As you might expect, a descriptive essay "describes" ideas and examples focused on a particular subject. It attempts neither to argue nor to persuade. Rather, it presents an impression—*your* impression—of something, through details that evoke one of the five senses.

When you are writing a text that's entirely descriptive, you use vivid language to make whatever you are describing come alive. Indeed, readers typically "visualize" what they read, and so any manner in which you can help them along makes for a stronger essay.

Descriptive essays fall into two broad categories: objective and subjective. Objective essays describe the topic in a literal, impartial way. As much as is possible, the writer's feelings are not revealed. These types of essays tend to include words that don't convey a high degree of emotion.

Subjective essays, on the other hand, communicate the writer's opinion; their intention is to evoke from the reader an emotional response, among other things. These types of essays use words charged with some emotional tone and a clear-cut attitude.

There are several elements to a descriptive essay. Above all, it should use words that appeal to the five senses: smell, touch, hearing, taste, or feeling. Does your subject make noise? Does it have a specific feel when you touch it? Can you taste it? Of course, you won't be able to—and it's not necessary to—apply all five senses to every subject you write about, but strive to use as many as you can.

DON'T WRITE ONLY ABOUT WHAT YOU SEE OR HEAR

Too often, we focus on describing things that we see or hear. Think about how words related to touch, smell, and taste create instant pictures: *itch*, *rub*, *sting*, and *whiff*.

Use Precise and Vivid Language

Successful descriptive essays use words that come alive. Think of yourself as a painter whose canvas is the paper. Words can create pictures and impressions that appeal not only to the mind but also to the five senses. Use words and phrases that will turn the words on a flat page into a sensory experience for the reader. Bring out textures, colors, tastes, sights, sounds, and smells. Use striking adjectives, active verbs and other vivid details to present your scenario and create sharp mental pictures.

The way you do this is to select highly specific words. This isn't necessary in every sentence—in fact that would be distracting—but you want to do it where possible. "He thought about the problem" is far less specific than "He pondered the problem for five days but was still unable to come up with a resolution that would satisfy everyone."

USE WORDS THAT CONJURE UP IMAGES

Judgmental words such as *angered*, *offensive*, or *unsympathetic* tend to defeat the purpose of a descriptive essay. Use them sparingly. Instead, create images through your words.

Include Imagery

Similes and metaphors make comparisons to enhance the reader's understanding of an experience or event. They create instant visual images in the reader's mind. Similes are comparisons using *like* or *as*, whereas metaphors are direct comparative statements, usually using *is*.

Original sentence: "He was angry."

Modified: "He felt like a hornet was buzzing in his head."

Simile: Anger is compared to a hornet.

Original sentence: "It snowed heavily."

Modified: "The white blanket covered the city in silence."

Metaphor: Snow is compared to a white blanket.

Original sentence: "Her eyes were greenish."

Modified: "Her eyes flashed like emeralds."

Simile: Green eyes are compared to emeralds.

Original sentence: "She walked down the street unsteadily."

Modified: "She wobbled like a wounded duck."

Simile: Her gait is compared to a duck's.

COMPARISON CAN BE A HELPFUL TOOL

When you write, "he cackled like a hyena," you create an immediate impression. Comparison makes for a clear visual image when you compare your subject to something else.

"Show, Don't Tell"

The emphasis on both precise language and imagery can be summarized in this simple rule for description: The most important part of a descriptive essay is the picture you create in the mind of the reader. Your goal is to infuse your experience into the mind of your audience.

In order to affect a permanent image on the part of the reader, your description must be specific to the situation at hand. You must draw readers into your world. Remember, the key principle of description is to "show, don't tell." As you write, use vivid sensory details, which change the flat "telling" of a story into "showing."

SPECIFIC IS ALWAYS BETTER THAN VAGUE

Students often feel that it's safer to use vague language. In fact, that just weakens your writing. Choose concrete and specific words over general and vague words.

Consider these two pairs of sentences. Each pair refers to the same event.

A. He was in a lot of trouble and it looked like it would be difficult to escape.

B. He was hanging over the rocky face of a cliff, scrambling for a handhold.

C. Her car crashed suddenly and it was totally destroyed.

D. The convertible careened sideways on two screeching tires, and then, smashing through the metal guardrail and into the cement abutment, it broke into two twisted pieces.

Clearly, the second sentence in each pair is more descriptive: The sensory details evoke our sense of sight, noise, and touch—thus creating a more realistic scenario.

Rules to Follow

Following are some basic rules to keep in mind as you write a descriptive essay.

Topic: If you are not specifically given a topic, you must decide on one. Brainstorm three or four experiences that have made an impression on you. Of these, which has the best potential for creating vivid images and striking sensory impressions? You may wish to seek feedback from a peer or teacher. Quite often, the act of discussion clarifies the task of which topic to select.

Put words on paper: Begin writing about your chosen experience. But keep in mind that you don't have to start at the beginning! Pick any place in the course of the experience that stands out to you. Put that down on paper. Later on, you'll add to that sequence of events, rounding out what happened beforehand and after. For now, you just need something written to work with. One technique is to write without stopping as much as you can in 10 or 15 minutes. Write without editing; get a flow of ideas going on paper!

Review and organize your draft: Outline or in some way plan the organization of this experience, event, character, or picture. Think about how to present the details, where to begin, and how to end. Employ transitions: many writers confuse their readers by not using words that connect the content of one paragraph with the next. Then, rewrite.

Apply descriptive craftsmanship: This is the step in which you apply what you have learned about showing not telling. Review your work and then try replacing some of the more non-descriptive words with more vivid imagery. Use a thesaurus if you'd like (but don't simply insert words that are unfamiliar to you). Make sure your language is precise and evocative: Use similes and/or metaphors to enhance the pictures you've created.

Though it isn't necessary to write about all five senses, use as many as are appropriate. Check back to see how many of your paragraphs contain sensory examples. Work through them line by line and decide how you can make the impressions more striking and intense.

Do a final review: Review your opening paragraph: Do you begin with an important attention-getter? After reading your first line, will the reader want to continue? Check your conclusion. Do you leave the reader with a lasting impression?

A Model of Descriptive Writing

The essay below, excerpted from its original form, commemorates the first anniversary of the 9-11 attacks on the World Trade Center. The language and imagery make it highly engrossing. As you read, underline the examples that, in your opinion, stand out.

FIVE WHO SURVIVED

Up, or down?
Kelly Reyher stood in the crowded 78th-floor elevator lobby of World Trade Center 2 and pondered whether to retrieve his Palm handheld from his office, 22 stories above. It was just after 9 A.M. on September 11, 2001, and Reyher, a lawyer with Aon Risk Services, had been interrupted in mid-evacuation. Fifteen minutes earlier a Boeing 767 had flown into the North Tower, touching off a fireball that, across the 140 feet separating the buildings and through the windows on the 103d floor, still felt to one of Reyher's colleagues, Judy Wein, "like putting your head in an oven." Reyher and about 20 co-workers had set off down the stairs, then turned around after hearing an announcement that the South Tower was "secure" and workers could return to their offices.

They had emerged on 78, one of two "sky lobbies" where workers transferred between express elevators to the street and local cars serving the floors above. At that moment a second 767 was banking over New York Harbor on a course that would lead it to within 100 feet of where Reyher was standing. To anyone who could have seen the disaster in the making, the right decision was self-evident: go down. Reyher, 41, watched as his colleagues piled into a car headed for the street. Then he punched the button to go up.

3   Up or down, life or death. The two great fires in the sky touched off by the 9-11 terrorists swept everything before them—paper and plastic, concrete and steel, flesh and blood. At least 1,100 people were trapped on or above the floors where the planes struck—roughly from 78 and above in the South Tower, and 94 and up in the North. Some jumped to their death; others tried to reach the roof (which was locked) in hope of a rescue by helicopter (which authorities had ruled out anyway), or waited for emergency workers, who never reached them. But a tiny handful—fewer than 20, according to definitive surveys by *USA Today* and The New York *Times*—made their way down a smoke-filled and treacherous stairway in the South Tower to safety. Of the 17 still alive, 10 agreed to tell their stories to *Newsweek*, some for the first time. ... They brought with them indelible memories of wrecked hallways lined with corpses, and a humbling awareness of how narrowly they slipped through the door to survival. Because those who lived weren't the smartest, or fittest, or best prepared, and as a group they were no more deserving of life than the firefighters who passed them on the stairs going up. The key to survival wasn't even as simple as knowing in which direction the street lay. Just ask Kelly Reyher.

What many of them recall is how dark it was afterward, and how still. There were, by various estimates, as many as 200 people crowding the sky lobby when the 767 smashed into the south face of Tower 2, flying in a steep bank that spanned seven stories. Wein, 45, was there with three colleagues from Aon and, in a separate group, Ling Young, 49, and Mary Jos, 53, college friends who worked together in the New York State Department of Taxation and Finance. The blast wave from the plane's impact, channeled between the elevator banks, swept north up the central lobby where people were waiting, and leveled them. "I flew from one side of the floor to the other side," Young recalls. "When I got up I had to push things off me. I can't see because my glasses were filled with blood. I took them off, cleaned them very carefully, and I looked around and saw everybody lying there, not moving. It was like a flat land. Everybody was lying down."

With the initial impact, Wein went flying, too, and was airborne long enough to reflect on what a crummy, meaningless way to die this was. She landed on her right forearm, shattering the ulna almost beyond repair. Then, as the tower shuddered and snapped back to the vertical, she slid back across the floor in a jumble of debris, coming to a stop just short of an open elevator shaft through which she could see flames licking up from below. "I got up and walked to the people in my group, walking over bodies. They were all over. I sat down, and Howard [Kestenbaum], my boss, was flat on his back and motionless, and I believe he was not alive. I've known him for 23 years." She remembered that there was a communications desk in the middle of the floor and she went to find it, but it was gone, and the farther south she walked the more bodies she encountered. Men in suits sat amid the wreckage of marble walls and ceiling tile, crying softly. She walked back toward the north windows, where she could see papers fluttering from the burning North Tower, and she sat down on the floor to wait. ...

Six floors above the sky lobby, Richard Fern, 39, a technical-support manager for Euro Brokers, remembers watching people jump from the windows of the North Tower and thinking, it's about time I got out of here. He had just stepped into an elevator that would take him down to 78 when the second plane hit, tossing him against the wall of the car and knocking him to his knees. He got up and scrambled for the nearest exit, which turned out to be Stairway A. It was dark inside and he could smell smoke, but he could just make out a luminescent stripe on the steps, and there was never any doubt in his mind about which way to go: down. "I'm running and running, and all of a sudden there's a man and a woman looking up at me saying, 'You can't pass.' There was a wall down, and it was covering the staircase. I didn't even acknowledge them or say anything; I just lifted the wall a foot or so, and it popped onto the handrail and stayed there, and I went underneath. I hope they followed me." A little farther along he came to another section of collapsed wall, and this time he went over it, skidding and rolling down and landing on his feet. Farther down, the stairs were clear but still seemed to stretch endlessly. "When I got down to the 30s my legs just felt like lead. But I didn't take a break, not once. All I could think was 'Get out, get out.'"

Just behind Fern another group left the 84th floor, composed of six or seven men led by Brian Clark, a 54-year-old executive vice president of Euro Brokers. Three floors down they encountered a man and a woman, probably the same pair who had accosted Fern. The woman—Clark remembers her as "very heavy" and her companion as "frail"—urged them to turn around and head back up. "You can't go down!" she warned. "There's flames and smoke. We've got to climb higher, to get above it." While the group debated what to do, Clark heard a banging from the other side of the stairway wall, and a voice calling for help. He squeezed through the partially blocked doorway leading to the 81st floor. The last thing Clark saw on the stairway was his companions Bobby Coll and Kevin York and David Vera, calming the woman, taking her by the elbows and helping her up the steps, away from the fire. They all died.

The man calling for help was Stanley Praimnath, 45, an executive at Fuji Bank who had improbably survived an almost head-on collision with the jetliner. ... He was answering a phone call when he saw the nose of United Airlines Flight 175 filling his window. He dropped the phone and dived to the floor just before the plane hit—Praimnath calculates barely 20 feet away.

The floor was a shoulder-high heap of rubble, and Praimnath could smell the jet fuel boiling out of the ruptured tanks. He hauled himself to the top of the wreckage and began to crawl away from the gaping hole made by the fuselage. He heard voices, saw Clark's flashlight and let out a yell.

Now smoke was beginning to envelop them. Praimnath was having trouble breathing. But Clark found himself—"miraculously," he says—in a "bubble" of fresh air.

Praimnath was still separated from his rescuer by an eight-foot-high slab of wallboard.

"Do you believe in Jesus Christ?" he yelled to Clark.

That's not what Clark expected to be asked, but he said he did.

Praimnath asked Clark to pray with him, and they shared what Praimnath describes as a moment of reverent silence, although what Clark remembers thinking was "Let's get the hell out of here!"

"I pointed a finger at him and I said, 'You must jump over this! It's the only way out!' He jumped, got a handhold, and I tried to grab him, but I missed. He went up again and somehow I got an arm around his neck and pulled him up and over."

The two men, remarkably uninjured save for bloodied palms, walked down 81 flights and out to the street, where they headed for Trinity Church.

"You saved my life," Praimnath exclaimed fervently.

"Well, Stanley," Clark replied, "maybe so. But you may have saved my life too." He didn't realize, at that moment, how true that was. As they watched, the tower plummeted to the ground. ...

And that leaves Kelly Reyher in his elevator on the 78th floor, the man who chose to go up when the smart people were heading down. But the colleagues who boarded an express elevator for the 45-second trip to safety never arrived downstairs. As for Reyher, he was knocked unconscious by the jolt and came to in a wrecked car in a burning shaft. He squeezed through a narrow gap between the doors, using his briefcase as a shield against the flames, and then, with his colleagues Keating Crown and Donna Spera, made his way down Staircase A to safety. And the very next day he drove far out on Long Island with his fiancée, Liz, and her 18-month-old daughter, Caitlin. It was as he watched Caitlin splashing in the pool that he cried for the first time, over the randomness of his survival, the preciousness of what he had nearly lost and the magnitude of the grief settling over the nation. And it is that which has stayed with him and sustained him through this terrible year, the laughing girl in the pool, a reminder of the moment when, on a sunny, terrible morning in New York, he somehow chose life.

—Jerry Adler, *Newsweek*, September 11, 2002

This essay is an example of the power of vivid description: It provides extensive detail on a harrowing experience. The sections below will discuss a handful of significant examples.

Paragraph 3

All of the words combine to describe the picture of the horrific power of the fire. The details give life to the paragraph and prepare us for what is to come.

We're led to a picture of a holocaust that killed all but a very few. Those few survived the trek "down a smoke-filled and treacherous stairway" (a phrase much more gripping than *down the stairs*).

Descriptive details are included, balancing the phrasing with a point-counterpoint "paper and plastic, concrete and steel, flesh and blood."

The final sentence creates a sense of suspense, leading us to wonder Reyher's fate, which we do not learn until the end of the article. (A photograph accompanying the opening of the article made it clear that he survived.)

Paragraph 5

Shattering the ulna almost beyond repair. The author could have simply stated, "severely breaking her arm." But the word *shattering* is more evocative than *breaking*; the word *ulna* identifies a specific bone in the arm.

The tower shuddered. Note here the power of anthropomorphism: By making the building shudder, the building is given humanlike qualities, expressing fear as well as the actual "shaking."

Jumble of debris gives a clearer picture than *mess*.

Flames licking compares the fire to an animal and creates an image of "tongues" of fire. It is more precise than to say *flames rose up*. It is an example of *showing*, not telling.

Paragraph 6

Scrambled for the nearest exit elicits an image of a person running through a chaotic scene. To say he *searched* or *ran* for the nearest exit would not capture the essence of *scrambled*.

Luminescent stripe tells the reader not only that the line was bright, but that it was glowing in the dark.

Skidding and rolling down the wall makes the reader visualize exactly how Fern managed to get over the wall, in a way that *jumping over* or *rumbling through* would have failed to convey.

Paragraph 9

Praimnath could smell the jet fuel boiling out of the ruptured tanks. It's possible that all Praimnath may have said was that he smelled gas. But by clarifying the source of the actual smell, the author makes a connection that readers might not have made. It also further advances the urgency of the situation.

Gaping hole made by the fuselage. This phrase might have otherwise been *The opening made by the airplane.* But the search for the right words yields a much more precise, clear sentence. The author knew that that this wasn't just any opening—it was indeed a gaping hole. And from the information in paragraph 9, the author could be more precise in stating the hole was created by the fuselage—the tube-shaped "body" of the airplane.

Look back at the first three words of the essay: You'll see a simple question. This question "Up, or down?" serves as a metaphor for the entire article. Indeed, it reflects the arbitrary nature of the decisions that led some people to safety and others to death. In paragraph three, we read more about this metaphor, with some clarification: The nature of the choice was, "Up or down, life or death."

And again, in the final paragraph, the author returns to the metaphor of an up-or-down choice, framing the article and providing a cohesive conclusion. Not a summary of the first few paragraphs, the conclusion returns in the final line to the article's central idea: the survival issue. The final image of the "laughing girl in the pool" completes the picture—it is a powerful symbol of what the victims had lost and of what the survivor is now able to treasure. The final sentence emphatically closes the story.

The Narrative Essay

Narration is storytelling. Whether it tells a true story or fiction, a narrative essay gives an account of one or more experiences. It tells a story to make a point or explain an idea or event. As a result, this type of essay can be fun to read and even to write. Usually personal and often autobiographical, a narrative typically contains action, dialogue, elaborate details, and/or humor.

Narrative essays work best when centered on a single episode of significance to the author. In such cases, the challenge is to make the significance appealing—even important—to others. While inexperienced writers might assume that newsworthy events are what one logically should write about, most of us don't experience newsworthy events. The experienced narrative writer takes what happens every day—whether interesting or funny or touching—and finds a way to make it something to share with an audience beyond friends and family.

Because of its story-like nature, the narrative is not typical of most essays. It does not require the standard thesis sentence stating your main idea, nor does it require the traditional introduction, body, or conclusion—though it is certainly fine to include those items. This is not to say that your essay does not require a strong theme—indeed it does—but it does not have to be stated in the traditional, highly defined way. Your theme might be a lesson you have learned. It might be an awareness you have made.

DON'T OVERUSE *I*

A narrative is typically written in the first person (*I* did this or that), but don't go overboard. Not every sentence–or even every other sentence–should include *I*.

All narratives have certain elements in common. They:

- Unfold over time
- Have characters that display some type of emotion
- Center on events more than ideas

Let Your Essay Unfold Over Time

Time (chronological order) is most often the organizing principle in a narrative essay. Stories and events happen in a certain order, and this order must be communicated to the reader. Events or experiences are listed in sequence of how they happened. With some narratives that focus on an emotion or a person, a flashback technique might work best. Just be sure to sequence your material in some type of logical order.

Achilike uses chronological order to advantage, moving through time from embarrassment to pride in her name. Specific scenes are set—in time and in place—and recreated for the reader. Her essay begins with her wish that she had a "cool name." In Paragraph 4, she uses a flashback scene to relate her first awareness of her unusual name. Then, she relates her feelings about it and moves forward to her discovery of its meaning. The reader easily moves with her, following a clear sequence of time and events.

Display Emotion

A good narrative essay connects readers to some sort of emotion felt by the essay's subject. When you read the header *Display Emotion* above, anger, sadness, pain, or joy may have come to mind. They're naturally the first emotions we think of, but they're also extremes.

171

Many other, equally compelling, emotions merit elaboration: jealousy, perseverance, loneliness, anxiety, and passion to name a few. Though these feelings are often more subtle and harder to articulate, they are powerful. If you can incorporate them into your essay, your writing will be stronger. Feelings are the prime vehicle for creating an instant reaction on the part of your reader. They're what we all identify with.

In paragraph 4, Achilike describes her humiliation and embarrassment by saying, "I found myself wishing I could sink into the ground and never come back." As readers, we can connect with these emotions because we all have experienced them.

DETAILS ARE IMPORTANT

> Achilike uses the following details to illustrate her feelings of loneliness: "…all the other girls in my class had sparkly, pink pencils with their names printed on them. You know, the ones they sell in the stores along with name-embossed sharpeners, rulers and pencil pouches. …I could never find a pencil with my name on it.

The simple details of "sparkly pink pencils" present a vivid poignant image of a girl feeling alone and isolated from her classmates by a name that she can never find printed on the items the other girls used. The details bring her emotions alive in a way that simply stating "I felt so alone…" never could achieve.

Here's another example. This time, the writer shows his emotions about a common experience: choosing which college to attend. The text presented here is his opening paragraph.

> When I applied under Early Decision to the University of Pennsylvania four years ago, I was motivated by two powerful emotions: ambition and fear. The ambition was to fulfill my lifelong expectation of attending an Ivy League school; the fear was

> that without the advantage offered by Early Decision, I wouldn't make the cut. A Penn admissions officer told me that the previous year they had accepted 45 percent of Early Decisions applicants and just 29 percent of total applicants. The implication was clear: applying under Early Decision dramatically improves your chances of acceptance. At Brown University, my other favorite, applying early did not confer any advantage. While Brown was my No. 1 choice, Penn was a close second, and I desperately wanted to make sure I got into one of the two.
>
> —Ben Adler, *Newsweek*, from "Better Think Before You Apply,"
> November 18, 2002

Choosing to start out with a direct statement, the author defines the event straight away. We know immediately how he felt and, along with a bit more detail as to what happened, the stage is effectively set for what's to come.

Often, the emotion that is shared in a narrative—or really in any type of story—is done to tell a bigger story. The narrative part of the essay serves as a link to the big picture. Consider the beloved fairy tale *The Three Little Pigs*. While children love reading about the pigs and the big bad wolf, the tale manages to impart a not-so-subtle message: it pays to be prepared. The narrative, therefore, serves as a vehicle for delivering the larger lesson.

Use Anecdotes

Anecdotes (short accounts of interesting events) are a good way to make your thoughts more concrete to the reader.

In the essay, "Why Couldn't I Have Been Named Ashley?" Achilike uses the anecdote particularly well in paragraph 7, which includes precise descriptions of the dialogue and scene in which her cousin tells her what her Nigerian name means.

We can visualize the two girls learning to be friends, and the negative shock when the author thinks her cousin is making fun of her. Then, as her cousin's words sink in, we can identify with her pleased astonishment. She has managed to include the reader in her important discovery of the significance of her name.

The anecdote leads directly to her concluding reflections on the meaning of her narration for herself and, by inference, for others. She has learned that her name means something: it has a proud history. She is not isolated; she is part of a worthwhile family, and she no longer feels humiliated because her name is not a common one.

Center on Events

As we have said, a narrative tells a story. But more precisely, it is a story that recounts events as they happened—in order to make a point. You aren't just reporting the details of what happened, you want to apply a broader meaning to the event. In order to do this effectively, you must focus on events more than ideas.

Whether you start in the middle of story or at the beginning doesn't matter. You want to focus on the events that were meaningful to you. The shorter the time-span you write about, the narrower your focus will be.

> **DON'T TAKE THE CONCEPT OF AN EVENT TOO LITERALLY**
>
> Yes, most often narratives focus on a specific episode in time, but the focus can also be a feeling you experienced in time. Just remember the events that prompted you to feel that way.

Stories should be described in the same way that they developed. This will ensure that your reader understands how and when things happened. This doesn't mean just reciting the events in sequential order as if you're reading a list, though. Pick and choose your details. While you want to convey the full imagery of the story, too many details will be distracting.

As you describe your story in the manner in which it happened, make sure you keep your verb tense consistent and clear. Reread your work several times to make sure that there is no confusion about when things happened and what you might be feeling now.

Rules to Follow

Consider the following questions when you think about a topic. Maybe there was a time that things didn't turn out as expected. Maybe you recently had a great accomplishment. Maybe you witnessed something troublesome.

- What happened? In what order did it happen?
- Who was involved?
- Where were you?
- How did you feel? Was there something to be learned from the experience?

Now clarify the two most important things about this event: the sequence of what happened and the way you felt. Think about how you will make what you felt emotionally real to your readers. Write a list of words that create a picture in your head—words that bring colorful details to mind. Then, draw on your word bank to start writing your essay.

A Model of Narrative Writing

The following essay does exactly what a narrative is supposed to do: It tells an interesting story with clarity, simplicity and emotion. The author shares her feelings about her unusual name as she narrates the growth in her understanding of what it means to her.

Why Couldn't I Have Been Named Ashley?

"Ashley!" exclaimed Mrs. Renfro, and simultaneously three heads whipped around at attention towards the perturbed teacher. At the same time, all three Ashleys proudly replied, "Yes, ma'am?"

When I was a fourth grader, I remember sitting in class that day just before the bell rang for dismissal. I remember thinking of all the names in the world, how could I have possibly been stuck with such an alien one. I thought about all the popular kids in the class. I figured that I wasn't popular because of my weird name. I put some things together in my mind and came up with a plausible equation: COOL NAME = POPULARITY. The dismissal bell rang. As I mechanically walked out to catch my ride, I thought to myself, "Why couldn't I have been named Ashley?"

I was born, on July 7th, 1986, in Parkland Hospital of Dallas, Texas. I was the first American-born Nigerian in both of my parents' families. I was my parents' first joy, and in their joy, they gave me the name that would haunt me for the rest of my life, Immaculeta Uzoma Achilike.

The first time I actually became aware of my name was on the first day of first grade. I went to school loaded with all my school supplies and excited to see all of my old kindergarten friends. I couldn't wait to see who my new teacher was. As I walked into the classroom, all my friends pushed up to me, cooing my name: "Imma, Imma, I missed you so much." The teacher walked in with the attendance sheet. She told everyone to quiet down so she could call roll. Before she started, she said something I thought would have never applied to me. She said, "Before I call roll, I apologize if I mispronounce anyone's name," with a very apologetic look on her face. She looked down at the attendance sheet, paused for a minute, and then looked up with an extremely puzzled look on her face. I remember thinking that there was probably some weird name before mine, although my name was always the first one to be called in kindergarten. Suddenly, my palms started sweating and then she began to hopelessly stutter my name, "Im-Immaculet Ach-liki, I mean, Achei..." My ears burned with embarrassment and droplets of perspiration formed on my nose. "Did I say it right?" she said with the same apologetic look on her face. Before I responded, the laughs that the other kids in class had been holding back suddenly exploded, like a volatile vial of glycerin, into peals of laughter. One kid thought it was so funny his chubby face started turning red and I could see a tear gradually making its way down his face. I found myself wishing I could sink into the ground and never come back. I hated being the laughing stock.

I never really recovered from the shock of that day. From that day forward, the first day of school was always my most feared day. I didn't know what to do; all I could do was tell my teachers, "I go by Imma."

I felt so alone when all the other girls in my class had sparkly, pink pencils with their names printed on them. You know, the ones they sell in the stores along with name-embossed sharpeners, rulers and pencil pouches. Every year I searched through and rummaged around that rack at the store, but I could never find a pencil with my name on it.

The summer of my seventh-grade year, my family and I took a vacation to our "home" in Nigeria, where my parents were born. My cousin and I were playing cards, talking girl talk, and relating our most embarrassing moments. Each tried to see whose story could top whose. I told one story of how I wet the bed at a sleepover, and she told me how she had farted in class during a test. That was a hoot. Then, I told her the story of how I was laughed at because of my weird name. I thought it was pretty funny, but she didn't laugh. She had the most serious look on her face, then she asked me, "Immaculeta Uzoma Achilike—do you know what your name means?" I shook my head at her and that's when she started laughing. I thought she was making fun of me, and as I started to leave she said: "Immaculeta means purity, Uzoma means 'the good road' and…". Having heard her words, I turned around in amazement. "What does Achilike mean?" I asked. After a long pause she said, "Achilike means to rule without force." I was astonished and pleased. I never knew what my name meant.

My name is Immaculeta Uzoma Achilike. I am the daughter of first-generation Nigerian immigrants. I am the daughter of hardworking and brave parents. My name means "to rule without force." My grandfather was a wealthy man of generous character. When I say my name in Nigeria, people know me as the granddaughter of a wealthy man of generous character. They know me by my name. There my name is not embossed on any pencil or vanity plate. It is etched in the minds of the people.

My name is Immaculeta Uzoma Achilike.

—Imma Achilike, second-place winner, 2004 Kaplan/*Newsweek* "My Turn" Essay Competition

The Personal Essay

Most essays are personal in one way or another. There is one type of essay, however, whose entire focus is on you: the personal essay. Personal statements are demanded by colleges because they are perhaps the best way to get to know you. In fact, a well-written personal statement may reveal more about you than an interview. With an essay on paper, you aren't burdened by someone else's questions—you set the tone, you decide the content, and you revise as you would like.

On a more global scale, the purpose of a personal essay is to present your own insight about things that have affected you. At the same time, since the personal essay is more than just a private journal, it must appeal to the reader at large. The personal essay, therefore, should be interesting and relevant to a larger world.

A personal essay is more informal than the other types of essays we have discussed. Because it is your own creative writing, there are far more liberties you can take for expressing yourself. It may be less formulaic and more offbeat than an academic essay. It may be more emotional, too. At the very least, it is more conversational in tone than other types of essays.

One kind of personal essay presents your reflections on an important experience. For this, you'll want to focus on how and why the events you are writing about have shaped your ideas, perspective, and insight. If you are writing for a general audience, you'll want to describe the experiences that led you to your thought-provoking ideas.

What goes into your personal essay depends on your audience. The more you know about that audience, the more effective your personal essay will be.

HAVE A RELIABLE IMAGE OF YOUR AUDIENCE

If you know who will be reading your personal essay, you can direct the tone and put it in context. Your essay will come across as more focused and you will be rewarded with an audience that is interested in knowing about you.

Show Personal Growth and Insight

A main feature of the personal essay is the examination of personal growth and reflection upon it. Reveal something important—maybe vulnerable— about yourself. "You Can Call me the Silver-Tongued Frog," in Chapter 2, has many elements of a personal essay and includes the author's descriptions of his vulnerability as well as reflections on his personal growth.

Don't feel that your topic has to be one of extreme hardship: It doesn't. There's no reason your experience has to be one of suffering or pain, such as a life-threatening illness or a family member's death. While those types of hardships can indeed inspire great change in people, it's also possible to be moved by the smaller things in life.

INCLUDE BOTH PERSONAL OPINIONS AND SOCIAL THEMES

The most interesting personal essays reveal how a private experience has implications for the lives of others. These might include family conflict, stereotyping, or societal problems.

Your essay doesn't have to be the most creative or most insightful, but it does have to propose a thought-provoking idea or sentiment. Don't rule out small occurrences and simple events that have prompted a new outlook in you. Those types of stories have as much power as the larger ones. Maybe you were affected by your first piano recital in front of a large group of people. Maybe you were affected by how your father takes the time every Saturday to play ball with you.

No matter what the topic, the question you should be asking is: How has this event made me feel and why is it important to me? As a rule, a narrow focus is more effective than a wide-ranging generalization. It's easier to stay on course when you are writing about one angle of something.

Stay away from topics such as, "I have always cared about people but began volunteering once my grandmother died." After all, everyone likes to think of himself as caring, so your writing about it won't make your topic unique. On the other hand, if there's an unusual twist that explains a new perspective, feel free to write about it.

Exude Confidence

The very nature of a personal essay means you're going to have to present yourself in a positive light. That's the point! Don't be embarrassed about this. In this type of essay, you will be writing about your achievements—either as an experience or as the result of reflection about your actions—so the tone of the essay will be positive.

However, don't be afraid to express your fears and doubts. We all have them. And learning how to deal with them makes each of us unique. Frequently, they become the basis for personal growth and achievement. Describing those relevant to your subject will make your essay more interesting and believable.

A Model of Personal Writing

The following essay recounts how one high school student was able to overcome her environment. Her concern is that her classmates haven't. She seems to have reflected long and hard about what has made it possible for her to succeed when none of her other classmates have been able to.

And I'm Watching it All from My Window

It was a typical Friday afternoon, and I was typically rushed. I was throwing on a T shirt, glossing over my hair and scanning the poem I would recite a few minutes later at La Pena, a cultural center downtown, when I caught a glimpse of the scene outside. Six or seven junior-high kids were walking down the street, the two boys in the rear yelling over the others' conversations. The girls had rolled up their shirts in the back to reveal pudgy midsections. As they stepped over condoms, around abandoned cars and past barking guard dogs, they joked and talked about who'd been shot and which of their friends was pregnant.

When I was in the sixth grade, I went to the public school in this neighborhood. I remember walking home with my classmates, having conversations similar to the one beneath my window. "Did you hear about Lisa's baby? Is she gonna stay in school?" We didn't always talk about kids we knew; rumors about friends of friends traveled through our group like rushing water.

By 11th grade, I had passed through several local school systems more affluent than West Oakland's as part of my parents' attempt to get me the best education possible. Getting older and hanging out

---

with a new crowd gave me a different perspective than the one I'd had as a sixth grader. Kids' getting shot was no longer some drama from which I could detach myself, or a joke to be shared with friends over sunflower seeds and Icees. It was real—hard deaths and stone poverty in my own community.

4 In five years, my block had changed. The boys from grade school were now men standing on the corner. Their eyes had grown increasingly red, their speech dense, their expressions more vacant. The forty-something women, mothers of girls my age, had become old and tired—secondhand mamas to their children's children.

5 Closest to my heart were the neighborhood girls who looked like they'd lost hope of ever knowing a better life. Girls I'd gone to school with at the age of 11 had become women at 15. Their stomachs sagged, their hands were full with diaper bags or money to push into the palms of the men on the corner. These were girls who walked like me; some even talked like me. But it was never me. I had things to do. I was on my way somewhere.

6 Dance class, gymnastics and writing workshops were some of the activities that kept me busy. I looked at the other girls on my street and saw that they were just as smart, pretty and capable as I was. I knew that the fundamental difference between us was that I'd been nurtured to expect only the best of life.

7 Unlike them, I never worried about whether my parents would make rent each month. I didn't wonder if I'd have to sell my flesh to feed my baby. I knew that the lights would be on when I sat down to write. Though money was, and still is, tight in my family, it's not my sole responsibility to make sense of it. I don't worry. Instead, I go to lectures at the University of California, Berkeley, or positive hip-hop concerts or workshops on body image and self-esteem.

8 Teachers, friends and family members have conspired to make sure that I know my potential. They have instilled in me a passion for living. Around here, the very fact that I recognize that I am special makes me special.

9 And I hate it. I shouldn't be unique. There shouldn't be a select few students who get to pursue happiness. West Oakland sits in the center of one of the most artistically and culturally diverse regions in the world, the San Francisco Bay Area. The neighborhood itself is

teeming with history, art and music. What if the kids I saw walking home from school were encouraged to go and listen to Bell Hooks speak? What if a teacher or parent pressed a Toni Morrison book into their hands? What if they had a safe space to write? They'd thrive.

10   The junior-high kids don't have the world at their fingertips simply because they've been taught, by circumstance, not to reach for it. As one of the fortunate few, I often feel like I don't deserve the joy of success. I wonder what my accomplishments mean when so many of my peers aren't achieving.

11   So that Friday, as I rushed to get out of the house, I couldn't help but stop and watch the kids in the street. One of the girls in the group looked a little like me. I'd seen her passing by before, but I had always averted my eyes. I can't stand the sight of a girl who doesn't know her own worth. But on this day I saw her, really saw her. I know her story, because it could have been mine. On that average afternoon, I decided to write—for her, for myself and for the hope of change.

—Chinaka Hodge, *Newsweek,* August 19, 2002
Second-place winner, Kaplan/*Newsweek* My Turn Essay Competition

Write about a Life-Changing Event

Many personal essay writers choose to write about a life-changing event. After all, an experience that affects you deeply will be something you can write about with ease. Present precise details of the event and lead the reader clearly through them toward a larger meaning. You want your audience to be able to feel why your reflections on it are important.

In the introduction to a personal essay for a general audience, you introduce yourself and set the stage for the major experience you plan to write about. This introduction needs to be brief and vivid. It serves the same purpose as the "lead-in" discussed in earlier chapters. If your readers are bored with the first paragraph, they may not give the rest of your essay much attention.

In the essay above, notice how much Hodge manages to reveal about herself and her neighborhood in her lead-in. She uses active verbs and vivid details to show us. In the first two sentences, we learn that amidst a scene typical of the community in which she lives, the author herself seems far from typical ("scanning the poem I would recite"). Immediately, we want to know more.

PRECISE LANGUAGE

Use action verbs, vivid descriptions, and dialogue that enhance the topic you are writing about.

"As they stepped over condoms, around abandoned cars and past barking guard dogs, they joked and talked about who'd been shot and which of their friends was pregnant." Hodge's ability to make us see the neighborhood she has lived in also make it possible for us to understand and think about the concerns and experiences that are important to her. Whatever type of personal essay you are writing, you want to have that effect on your reader.

Develop a Logical Order to Your Essay

Note, also, how the author above uses chronological order and combines it with community to create a transition between paragraphs 3 and 4: "It was real—hard deaths and stone poverty in my own community. In five years my block had changed." In paragraph 6, she lists activities she engaged in and suggests that the other girls on her street did not, then offers her reflections on why not. The real purpose of her essay emerges here.

Hodge's concluding paragraphs effectively refer back to her introduction. We are reminded of "that Friday" when the author saw the "junior high kids," and that it was precisely those kids who were the underlying concern of her essay: "...I often feel like I don't deserve the joy of success. I wonder what my accomplishments mean when so many of my peers aren't achieving." We also are reminded of how the author sees herself versus the kids around her, and understand her reflections on the meaning that has for her.

DEVELOPING YOUR PERSONAL ESSAY

In order to present yourself in the best possible light, you have to research yourself. Focus on your strengths, but—if necessary—provide a brief explanation of any weaknesses you think important to inform your audience about. Remember, one of the most efficient ways of gathering and organizing material is making lists to answer relevant questions.

- **What are my personal qualities?** (This is usually the hardest area, but list what you consider to be your strengths. Are you determined, honest, dependable, self-reliant, disciplined, creative? Have you overcome difficult social, emotional, or physical odds? Do you like to help people? Are you a natural leader? Do you explain things well?)
- **What experiences have I had that are significant to me and could be to others?** What have I learned from them? What can others learn?
- **Do I have any physical or health problems that are relevant to my audience and need defining or explaining?**
- **What passionate interests do I have?** (collecting, acting, creative writing, painting/drawing, building, outdoor interests, sports, special involvements)
- **What are my goals?** (academic, creative, job-related)
- **What are my academic successes?** (awards, difficult classes, test scores, grade point)

- **What extracurricular activities have I participated in?**
  (leadership positions, sports, clubs, school-related volunteer
  work such as tutoring)
- **What work experience have I had?** (Include job specifics,
  especially anything for which you were responsible.)
- **What community involvement have I experienced?**
  (church or youth groups, political action, organizations, etc.)

Review the lists you have for the above questions and think about
your audience. Will they want to know everything you've listed
under each question? Hopefully, you have a great deal you could say;
the question is, should you say it all? Probably not. Include only those
details you think will be important to the people for whom you are
writing.

Your essay may need to answer the question: "Why should we accept
you?" or "Why should we hire you?" or "Why should I read what you
have to say?" So you need to focus on explaining your strengths and
talents and/or your important ideas to the people who will read your
essay. Be as creative as possible in promoting yourself.

Your paragraphs will need to be organized into a logical order that
emphasizes the importance of whatever you want your readers to
know about yourself and/or your convictions. If your essay deals
with how you feel and/or what you think about some aspect of your
life, you may want to choose an organization that describes that
aspect and then present your reflections on it. Use chronological
order whenever that is appropriate. Then, be sure each paragraph
contains a topic sentence and the details relevant to it as well as the
transitions connecting it.

Although the body of your essay will be focused on answering your
readers' question, "Why should we . . .?" your introduction might
speak to the question of what makes your audience special to you.
Why do you want to get into that specific college, or land that

particular job, or present your own unique point of view to your readers? Whether you choose to address that question or not, your introduction will need to catch your readers' attention.

The conclusion of a personal essay may be the most important part of that essay. You want to leave the reader with the best possible image of you as well as with an understanding of your conviction that what you have written should make a difference—in your life, or your readers' life, or both. Your conclusion, therefore, needs to emphasize the significance of what you have written.

Section III

STRATEGIES TO IMPROVE YOUR WRITING

CHAPTER FOURTEEN

How Feedback Can Help Your Writing

When you seek feedback about your writing, you inject a dose of reality into the picture. You find out for certain whether you are making yourself understood. Having spent hours on end developing an essay, you tend to lose objectivity. It's an inevitable part of the writing process, and it happens to all writers. Feedback helps you see your essay with a fresh eye.

TAKE A BREAK FROM YOUR ESSAY

The first thing you should do with respect to a fresh eye is to put your essay away for a set period of time. If you're not in a rush to get your essay done, tuck it out of view for a solid week or two. If you're tight on time, put it away for as long as you possibly can, even if it's only for two days.

The point is to take a complete break from your essay and get it out of your mind. That way, when you return to it, you'll have a new perspective. Errors will stand out more clearly, and confusing transitions will be more apparent.

SEEK THE ADVICE OF OTHERS

Certain parts of the writing process can be collaborative. Even though you are the sole writer and likewise solely responsible for your writing, it is perfectly acceptable and necessary for good writing to involve other people. Why? You may want to brainstorm topic ideas; you may want input about whether your topic is too broad or narrow; you may want feedback on your drafts as you polish your writing; you may want reassurance once the writing is completed that it's interesting and engaging. At several stages in the process you will want to have input from others on your writing.

> "Even though parents absolutely may not tinker, feel free to give copies to your friends and teachers. That is the way writers work. Anyone who thinks it is cheating to let her essay be critiqued by others should use this in her essay as an example of a charming character flaw."
>
> —Jay Mathews, from "Crunch Time for Grads"
> *Newsweek,* November 4, 2002

If you haven't already done so, try forming a writing group, a circle of people with whom you share your ideas, drafts, and finished writings. This group may be your friends, classmates, teachers, and/or parents. (Your parents must not tinker with your work, as writer Jay Mathews warns above, but they'll be able to pick up on things your friends don't, so it's useful to seek their feedback.) You want to include people who will bring a variety of perspectives and contribute candid and thorough feedback. Your classmates are likely to point out different things than will your parents or teachers, so having multiple perspectives can only help. Enlist people whose opinions you respect. Make sure you ask friends whom you admire and feel communicate well.

AVOID THE 'RED' PEN SYNDROME

Have you ever had a teacher who marked up your paper with lots of red-pen marks? Consequently, you stopped reading after the third or fourth correction. Maybe this happened more than once. But when all was said and done, did those numerous edits about a comma here and a spelling mistake there actually help you improve your writing?

Not likely. It probably even had the opposite effect. Instead of making you a better writer, those edits may have caused you to feel discouraged and more confused about what's correct. The experience may even have caused you to avoid writing altogether. Why write when it seems so terrible, right?

Having someone respond to your writing in a traditional way (with editing marks) can indeed be beneficial, but it's best done with some parameters. The key here is to give your chosen editor some guidance.

- First, ask your editor to use a green or blue pen. It may sound simplistic, but the truth is that red sends us right into a defensive mode.

- Second, and more important, ask your editor to focus on just a few recurring errors, specifically those that cause confusion in comprehension or grammar. Transitions might fall into that category.

- Third, ask your editor to read your entire essay through once without putting that green pen to the page—and to make marks and comments only on the second read.

- Fourth, encourage your editor to highlight the positives, too. Where are the strengths of the piece? There's a lot that can be learned from understanding your strengths.

READ YOUR WRITING ALOUD

Reading aloud is a technique used by writers to make written material come alive. Whether you're reading your own work or a peer is reciting your work back to you, hearing the words spoken allows you to concentrate on how the essay flows. Add to that facial and vocal expressions, as well as personal interpretation, and you get a full impression of how your reader will inevitably hear your words.

Reading aloud also can help you become a better writer during the various stages of the writing process. Listen carefully to how the words come alive—or not so alive—through voice intonation, pacing, and volume. With practice, you will begin to recognize your strengths and weaknesses as a writer from the sound of it orally. Do your sentences all sound alike? Vary the length or use different verbs. Do you need to stop mid-sentence to take a breath? That's a good clue it's a run-on and might be better broken into two sentences. Do the pauses feel awkward? Take a close look at where you've placed your commas. Is that a question or a statement? In general, does the essay sound right? Reading aloud can give you reassurance that what you wrote is in fact clear. Learn to listen—literally—to your voice as a writer.

In addition to reading aloud your own writing, listen to the way someone else reads it aloud. Often someone else will give your sentences emphasis or phrasing different from what you intended. While the person is reading, make notes of what sounds right and what sounds like it needs a little more work. When the person has finished reading, talk with her about what she thought, and make note of her comments and questions.

GET GUIDED FEEDBACK

One of the most effective ways to get feedback from your peers is to have questions prepared for them to answer. Let's say you had a difficult time writing your conclusion; you just couldn't figure out how to wrap it up. That "struggle" or difficulty would be something you'd want to ask your reader about: In the end, were you indeed clear about your point? Ask your reader to pay close attention to that part of the essay and to whether your point came through. Does it make her reflect on your position?

General questions:

> What is your reaction to my paper? Did it keep your interest?
>
> What am I trying to tell you? What do I most want you to learn?
>
> What bias do you think I have toward the topic?
>
> What are this paper's greatest strengths?
>
> Does it have any major weaknesses?
>
> What suggestions do you have to make the paper better?

Questions on overall meaning:

> Do you understand everything? Is there anything missing that you'd still be curious to know about the topic?
>
> Does my paper share anything new or does it simply restate the obvious?
>
> Am I trying to cover too much or too little?
>
> Are there enough details and personal experiences?
>
> Would you recommend someone else to read this? Why or why not?

ASK FOR A WRITTEN RESPONSE

Have you ever thought about having someone write you a long response to your writing? Try it. Email works well for this approach. Send someone your writing as an attachment and ask him to respond via email.

Below is an example of a written response from a writer's friend:

I liked your paper about how to fight obesity in the United States. You've got some great ideas about how to change the way Americans think about eating, like making a family commitment to avoid fast foods, like McDonald's or Burger King (although I'd sure miss my Big Macs!). The way you started your paper by talking about your dad's struggle with his weight really got my attention. It was a good personal story. I wanted to see how things worked out for him.

I had some trouble getting what you were after in some parts. I didn't really understand the paragraph where you say that lots of people are complacent with their overweight conditions. I think you're trying to say that it doesn't matter why a person is obese, and that, even if there's some "bizarre" fat virus, you believe no one should play the victim and throw in the towel. This isn't clear, and it sounds more like opinion than something backed up with facts. Maybe you can find a doctor or expert to quote, and be a little less "emotional" here.

The only grammar I saw (but I'm no expert) was that sometimes I have trouble telling when things are happening. For example, you wrote "When I go to shopping malls, I had trouble with my will power. I always find myself in the food court, eating what's not good for me." I'm not sure if you still have trouble with your will power or if this is completely in the past. If in your past, you might try starting "When I went to shopping malls,"—and then make sure all your verb tenses line up.

I'm glad I read your paper. I learned a lot about a sensible diet and staying healthy, even with so many "hazard-devils" out there trying to persuade us to "eat fast and fat." It was also really interesting to work on improving your paper—I feel like I might be able to do this with my own writing now, too.

Although there's no formula for responding to writing, you may wish to provide your reader with guidelines for longer responses:

- Share what you liked about the paper
- Express what was difficult to understand or what you struggled with
- Highlight a few grammar points that need to be corrected

Though it is helpful to hear what the reader found interesting or thought needed revision, it's important to have her explanation, too. Press her to explain why she responded as she did. This will help you decide whether to incorporate the suggestions. Remember, just because someone else provides commentary about the writing doesn't mean you have to accept that as fact. Still, you should listen carefully to all feedback, and if you still cannot make a decision about whether to make a specific revision, ask another person to read it and see what he says.

COLLABORATION VERSUS PLAGIARISM

Getting feedback on your writing is not plagiarism. As long as the work started with you and as long as the suggestions you receive don't include having someone else rewrite your work, you're not cheating.

PEER RESPONSE WORKSHEET

Use this sample worksheet to help guide your comments or suggestions.

1. Offer at least one positive response to the writing. What did you like best? Make sure you explain why it captured your attention.

2. Why do you think the writer chose this topic? Do you feel sufficiently convinced that this writer knows enough to write on the topic? Provide reasons.

3. Is there one detail you most clearly remember? Why do you think you have remembered it?

4. Provide the writer with one suggestion to improve the paper. Explain why you believe this improvement is needed. Remember, it is a suggestion that the writer may not incorporate.

5. What else would you like to know about in the writing? Is there any type of gap in information here?

6. Is the content meaningful and specific, or is it general and superficial? Explain.

7. Is the writing finished (i.e., ready to be published or turned in for a grade)?

CHAPTER FIFTEEN

Improving Your Essay with Vocabulary

A strong vocabulary is essential to being a good writer: It allows you to have a richer relationship with the world of ideas. The wider range of words you have, the easier it is to find precisely the right word for your needs. Having a strong vocabulary also makes you a more effective communicator. People appreciate ideas more fully when they are conveyed with a clear and direct intent. And on a broader scale, having the right words contributes to having the right thoughts: Language creates new ways of thinking.

In effect, expanding your knowledge of words means you're more able to keenly express your perspective. The more vocabulary words you are comfortable with, the more precise you can be about your thoughts.

NO FORMIDABLE WORDS NEEDED

Essays aren't judged by the fancy words they may or may not include. They're judged by how well ideas are expressed and whether they move the reader.

Here are four things you should keep in mind with respect to selecting the right words in writing:

- Expand your vocabulary
- Use active verbs and lively modifiers
- Keep it varied
- Keep it simple

EXPAND YOUR VOCABULARY

As you might suspect, one of the most basic ways to improve your writing is to learn more words. The more words you know, the more articulate you can be. More specifically:

- You can better discuss/describe a topic.
- Your writing has more credibility.
- Your ideas are taken more seriously.
- You increase your depth of knowledge.

Using the precise word can make the difference between being understood and misunderstood. Many words mean similar things, but there are almost always subtle differences. Even when you think something might be a synonym for something else, chances are that there's some distinction. You'll want to choose the word with the meaning that captures what you want to say. To do that, you've got to expand your vocabulary.

How do you expand your vocabulary? Read, read, and read some more. As you read, you'll come across new words, and that's the time to learn them.

We all come across words we don't recognize. It can happen in any type of text. But since few of us carry around a dictionary, we all have to compensate and try to figure out the words ourselves: We make educated guesses about what new words mean by considering their context.

Just what does *context* mean? It refers to the conditions in which something exists—the complete meaning of something. When you see a word or phrase that's not familiar, what's the first thing you usually do? You probably look at the surrounding words and phrases to help you figure out what the unknown word means. In other words, you look at the *context clues* to help you read between the lines.

When you look at context clues to define a word, one of two things will happen: you'll see what the word means straight away or you'll see indirect information that will help you infer what it means. Use the information—either within the sentence or around it—to figure out what's going on. Consider the following two examples:

> "But isolated, surrounded only by *sycophants*, Saddam may not know he has been defeated until American soldiers kick in his door."

> "U.S. intelligence does not expect Saddam's regular Army, which consists of some 300,000 demoralized, frightened *conscripts*, to put up much of a struggle."

> —Evan Thomas and John Barry, *Newsweek,* from
> "Saddam's War," March 17, 2003

In the first sentence, even if you don't know what *sycophants* means, it's possible to glean the meaning from the context. A careful reading of the sentence would lead you to understand that sycophants are people who would be reluctant to report bad news to someone who supervises them. Specifically, they are servile, self-seeking flatterers.

In the second sentence, to find out what *conscripts* means, you could break down the wording of the sentence and fill in the blank: "Army ... consists of ... conscripts." You may not realize that a *conscript* is one who is drafted into military service (as opposed to one who volunteers), but you'd be able to figure out that a conscript is a troop or soldier—enough information to make sense of the sentence if you're not near a dictionary.

USE ACTIVE VERBS AND LIVELY MODIFIERS

When you deconstruct a typical sentence, what are the most engaging parts? It isn't the nouns; it's the action words and modifiers—the verbs, adjectives, and adverbs—that enliven text. They tell us interesting things about subjects and objects, and they enable us to see them in action.

Going a step further, the active voice is more powerful than the passive voice. With an active voice, the subject performs the action expressed in the verb. With a passive voice, the subject receives the action. Look at the difference between these two simple sentences:

> Maria presented the research paper. (**active**)

> The research paper was presented by Maria. (**passive**)

The second sentence sounds awkward, doesn't it? That's because it's written in the passive voice, which by nature tends to be vague, long-winded, and uninteresting. The active voice is almost always more direct and less awkward. On rare occasions, you're better off using the passive voice, but as a general rule, stay away from this type of writing. You certainly wouldn't speak this way, so you shouldn't write this way either.

STICK TO ACTIVE VERBS

It isn't always appropriate to use active verbs—nor is it desirable—but when possible, try staying away from the verb forms *to be, to do, to have,* and *to go*.

For some reason, many students think the passive voice sounds more mature and objective than the active voice. That's not at all the case! Objectivity—and certainly not maturity—have nothing to do with the way the sentence is structured. Your goal, most likely, is to sound authoritative and objective—but you cannot compromise sounding natural as well.

Take any reputable magazine article. Chances are, it's the lively words that attract you, not the hard words. The two paragraphs below, for example, taken from a photography review, show how well-selected verbs and apt modifiers can make a piece of writing stand out.

An American Eye

Walker Evans's pictures of Southern main streets, tenant farmers, Saratoga in the rain, subway riders, rundown barbershops and peeling billboard posters supply most of our defining images of the Depression. For some of us, they have come to define how a photograph should look, period. Not coincidentally the man behind those photographs was a study in contradiction—the first tip that maybe those pictures aren't as simple as they seem. Although he was a thoroughgoing modernist and a devoted Francophile, he did more than almost anyone to dignify vernacular American art and architecture with his photographs. He was a dandy whose idea of heaven was a pair of handmade shoes, but he is most famous for his penetrating photographs of Depression-era sharecroppers. He was restless all his life, moving from one style to the next, mastering that and then moving on to something else. The miracle is that out of this seemingly aimless artistic nomadism came images of such defining clarity that the photographer and curator John Szarkowski was once moved to wonder rhetorically "whether Evans recorded the America of his youth, or invented it." ...

No matter how iconic Evans's images have become, their disturbing power remains undiminished. The portrait of Allie Mae Burroughs, a sharecropper's wife, is one of the last century's most unnerving works of art—and one of its most complicated. This is even more remarkable because it is one of the quietest, simplest-looking pictures imaginable. Evans keeps his angle as straight on as a passport photo, using available light that barely casts a shadow. The illusion is that the camera isn't there. But that was his genius: to take a picture with so few prompts that the viewer stares a little harder. Then you begin to notice the worry lines in her forehead, the

> way she bites her lower lip, the severity of her countenance. You sense something trapped about this woman, but also something resolute. Staring straight into the camera, she almost dares you to stare back. Your curiosity aroused, you want to see deeper, but at the same time, you feel uneasy, as though you've trespassed on someone's privacy.
>
> —Malcolm Jones, *Newsweek*, January 31, 2000

Strong verbs such as *supply, define, dignify, remains,* and *stares* help describe this famous photographer and his works. And specific modifiers help to ensure that we get a precise picture:

- **vernacular** (common)
- **penetrating** (incisive)
- **aimless nomadism** (meandering)
- **rhetorically** (in order to make a point)
- **unnerving** (disturbing)
- **resolute** (strong-willed)

If you were to replace the modifier used in the text with the alternative modifier listed in the parentheses, would it alter the meaning of the sentence? No, probably not. But the modifiers used here express the kind of life captured by the pictures and are more concise in meaning.

KEEP IT VARIED

Variety matters in writing. It matters a lot!

Don't repeat yourself. Sometimes, when you find the perfect word, it's tempting to use it again in the paragraph. Don't do it! The problem with words like *penetrating* and *unnerving* is that since they are so precise, repeating them suggests you've run out of new things to say.

Vary your sentence structure. It's boring to read the same type of sentence pattern over and over again. Come up with different ways to write a sentence. Subject plus verb plus object is far too overused.

> He went to the fast-food restaurant. He decided that he would have a milkshake and fries. The server took his order and then he waited for his number to be called.

Vary your sentence length. Long sentences are hard to read, but short sentences can seem abrupt. Make sure you use intersperse both types of sentences into your text. That way, you make sure the reader will stay engaged. (And check your long sentences carefully to avoid run-on sentences, a common problem with students.)

Sentences with active verbs tend to be shorter than sentences with passive verbs. If you're having trouble shortening a sentence, see whether you have used the active voice properly and rework it.

Spice up the wording! Ask yourself these questions when you're editing text that lacks punch:

1. Is this the best possible way to express this thought?
2. Is this the most precise word I could use here?
3. Does this sentence express exactly what I intend to say?

If the answers are no, come up with new words and phrases. Use a thesaurus if you must, but it's better to get in the habit of brainstorming for the perfect word. Quite often, the word you're looking for will be on the tip of your tongue.

Avoid excess. The overuse of polysyllabic words will distract from your main point. Readers will be turned off, not impressed. And if you're writing a college-entrance essay, the admissions counselor may think you're trying to show off. Your writing should include mostly everyday words, with a sprinkling of advanced vocabulary where appropriate.

KEEP IT SIMPLE

Your goal in learning more words is to be able to keenly express your perspective. The more vocabulary words you are comfortable with, the more precise you can be about your thoughts.

Having said that, most writing situations don't require a fancy word. In fact, using a sophisticated word can work against you: It can sound formal and stuffy, and if you don't really know what it means, you run the risk of misinforming and confusing the reader. Teachers and admissions counselors are not looking for stilted language. They'd much rather see more natural, simple language that's well-constructed and clear. Choosing a simple, well-toned "50-cent word" over a big "ten-dollar word" is often the best choice.

Also, if you try too hard to use sophisticated vocabulary:

- You may lose readers who don't have the language skills or patience to read the essay.
- You may cloud the meaning rather than enhance it if you have used the incorrect word.
- Readers may find you pompous rather than erudite.

If you're unsure whether to use a certain word, look it up or don't use it. It's better to use a simple—but still accurate—word than a fancy one that might be incorrect or misleading.

DON'T WORRY ABOUT SOUNDING AUTHORITATIVE

A strong applied vocabulary is clear, concise, and deceptively simple. Readers—teachers included—aren't looking for writing that sounds commanding. They want confidence and originality—not a high-brow tone.

While you want your language to be simple and clear, don't use language that's predictable. Don't say things like, "It was a growing experience" or "I learned to appreciate others." Those kinds of expressions have been so overused that they mean little these days. Be simple but be fresh.

CHAPTER SIXTEEN

Keeping a Journal

Writers have always used journals to record their thoughts and feelings. These reflections are often used as the basis of other kinds of writing: letters, news articles, essays, editorials, and stories. Journal writing is especially important because it encourages a love of writing and self-expression, free of the constraints imposed by an assigned topic.

As you probably know, a journal is a first-person record of personal thoughts and daily experiences. This record captures the immediacy of a situation because it is written as the story unfolds or just after it happens.

The difference between a journal and a diary is subtle. In general, a diary focuses on a documentation of day-to-day events, while a journal tends to include reflections and thoughts about events that aren't necessarily related to the writer's life. To look at it another way, a diary might chronicle your dates, activities with friends, and social life. A journal might include your thoughts about politics and the crisis in the Middle East. Journal and diary writing often overlap.

All writers reveal something about themselves through their writing. However, the process of self-revelation is nowhere more pronounced than in the writer's journal.

The characteristics of journal writing include the following:

- First-person narrator
- Freedom of expression
- Informal or colloquial (conversational) writing style
- Emotional content
- Self-revelatory nature

Journal writing is very much like freewriting. Here, you explore not only yourself and your life, but also different ways to communicate and express yourself.

WHY KEEP A JOURNAL?

Other than the obvious advantage of keeping a private book of thoughts, why else might you want to keep a journal? How might it help you in refining your essay-writing skills? How might it help you to become a better thinker?

A journal can be a first step in organizing your thoughts. You likely think about thousands of things in a given day. A journal can be viewed as a "diary of the mind"—a chronicle of what you're thinking. After you've maintained a journal for a month or so, you'll find it fascinating to review your thoughts and scrutinize them for signs of consistency. How have they evolved over time? What role have others played in your thinking? Without a journal, your thoughts are likely more limited to your most recent feelings: It's impossible to remember exactly how you felt each day if you haven't written it down.

A journal helps you chronicle events and develop an eye for detail. Think back to a memorable time for which you have no photos, video, or diary. Don't you wish you had some of those memories? A journal ensures that your life's defining moments are captured. You may not remember your first week of high school very well, short of a few basic details, but had you kept a journal, you could have had an invaluable resource for an essay today on the topic of "starting over." Such a journal would contain descriptions and a level of detail that are rarely retained solely in one's memory.

A journal can help you write your college-application essays. Those personal essays you're writing for college aren't just testing your ability to write; they're also intended to let the admissions people get to know you. A well-maintained journal will be filled with glimpses of your personality. When preparing a college-application essay, flesh out some of your best material or deepest thoughts in a more traditional essay format, and you'll be well on your way to a compelling piece of writing. It's a great source for ideas, especially when you've got writer's block. (Some of your writing may be too personal; it's obviously up to you what you choose to reveal.)

There are other ways that maintaining a journal can make you a better writer:

- A journal encourages you to be creative.
- A journal encourages you to create colorful descriptions of significant things in your life: influential people, trivial but memorable events, and questions about everyday things.

Journals are typically not intended for publication but maintaining one can be a powerful source of inspiration for future writings. Try, for at least a month, to maintain a journal where you write your thoughts, experiences, fears, and hopes on a regular basis. Then attempt to write a personal essay.

Use your journal to help you formulate your idea, your topic, and your theme. Remember—you're not required to divulge your inner-most thoughts, only the aspects of those thoughts that you're comfortable sharing. Your journal can help you to formulate interesting, engaging topics, explore their significance, and place them in a larger social context.

While reading the following diary excerpts, notice how the entries incorporate all the characteristics of journal writing (e.g., first-person narrator, freedom of expression, etc.).

Diary of a Job-Hunter

Day One: …I am a graduate M.B.A. and I'm looking for a job. What will become of me and my bright-eyed colleagues? Once upon a time, great job offers piled up like loose change: as soon as we got rid of some, more would come in. And that wasn't even the best of it. If we didn't want to work for someone else, it seemed relatively easy for us to raise millions in venture capital, hire a bunch of people and launch an IPO. No more. In Silicon Valley these days, you can't even give away barely-used office furniture to charity—the warehouses are already too full. Companies that make stuff are getting pummeled and the ones that don't are mostly gone…

I want a position where I can develop new markets and products and make them become a reality. I want to enjoy the company of the people I work with and learn from them, too. In the last three months I've met with roughly 80 industry executives, venture capitalists, Stanford alumni, former colleagues and friends in the industry. In each meeting, I have either reestablished an old relationship or forged a new one. But as of today, I have no formal offers of employment and more than $70,000 in business school debt. What, I ask you, is an M.B.A. to do?…

Day Two: About four years ago, my girlfriend told me with equal parts anger and love that all of my best energies were used up at work, leaving only leftovers for the rest of my life. The reality is that many, if not most, working people today spend more conscious time with work colleagues than with friends and loved ones…

I'm a little wiser now. I know I'll never find a perfect balance between the professional and the personal, but I'm committed to trying. I know that much of my time will be devoted to my career, but I need the work to give me something back in return. I want to be surrounded by people I can learn something from, and I want to make a difference. …

Day Four: Most people—especially economists—like to keep their options open. Two seems better than one; more seems safer than less. But when you're looking for a job, too many options can be a bad thing. This is my current struggle. How will I know when a job is the one? What if I turn down the one? And when should I stop looking? …

Almost everyone I've met in my job quest asks me why, after having spent a summer in venture capital, I'm not going back into the field full-time. After all, venture capital, especially for drug development and health care, is going strong.…

Don't get me wrong, I loved working for a VC firm. The lifestyle was reasonable, the pay unlimited and the company's outlook matched my own—what's not to like? But when they asked me to come back, it came down to a simple choice: Do I want to make stuff, or do I want to fund other people so they can make stuff? For me, the answer is simple: Right now, I want to make stuff…

The next offer was also appealing. The consulting firm I worked for gave me a loan for business school that would be forgiven if I returned to work for them after I graduated. We're talking $70,000 worth of debt, miraculously wiped away. Plus, I'd be working with a burgeoning biotechnology group along with two of my favorite mentors and a few of my closest friends. But my decision came down to the same thing: Do I want to make stuff or to help others make stuff? …

Day Five: I've enjoyed the opportunity to share a week of my job search with you. It's been a twisting path of observations, personal accounts, and reflections, but I hope you've found it interesting. As for me, I'm hoping to complete my job search in the next month. No matter what, I think these next few years will be amazing.

—Greg Yap, *Newsweek* Web exclusive, April 2001

Yap's diary provides a snapshot of a moment in time the way no other form of writing can do. As is the case with a snapshot photo, the journal gains value over time. Whatever job Yap took, he inevitably questioned whether he made the right move. That way, he had a clear idea why he made the decisions he did. Note the techniques he employs:

First-person perspective: Yap is clearly writing about himself, and specifically about an important decision he faces. His writing is not intended to be persuasive, however, unlike much of the first-person writing explored in this book. Instead, it's intended to be revelatory— to illustrate this important life experience.

Freedom of expression: Since he does not have the burden of arguing a point, Yap is free to express his thoughts on a range of aspects of the job search. This approach is not effective in traditional writing, but it works here because it mimics how the mind works!

Emotional content: Although Yap is privileged to be a Stanford M.B.A. with an undeniably bright future, he touches on several emotionally charged issues that anyone can relate to. Should he take a job that would effectively eliminate his college debt but might not be intellectually satisfying? Should he pursue his ambitions even if it means giving up time with friends and loved ones?

Self-revelatory nature: With just a few brief entries, Yap's personality comes through clearly. That's because his writing is filled with personal references and insights.

JOURNALS FOR REFLECTION AND EXPLORATION

In 2002, Kurt Cobain's journals and letters were published. Before Cobain's *Journals* was released, *Newsweek* published excerpts from it in the magazine. At that time, Mark Whitaker, *Newsweek*'s Editor, wrote:

Over the years, we've run many stories that document the awful toll of drug abuse. But I don't think we've ever published a more powerful anti-drug testament than this week's excerpt from Kurt Cobain's *Journals*.

... Warning: while funny and delightful in parts, the excerpt is not for the faint of heart. But we think it will be essential reading for anyone who cares about Nirvana's music—and a fascinating and sobering journey for any reader.

"Essential reading" is what Whitaker feels this is. This response, to personal writings most likely never intended for the public, proves the power of the piece.

Cobain was able to get to his first thoughts by writing freely in his journals, which is what makes them so powerful. They are real and raw: not overcooked with edits and third or fourth thoughts. Cobain's erratic spelling and grammar remained intact in *Journals*. He expresses isolation, passion, ambition, ambivalence, and caution. Cobain used journal writing for everything and anything going on in his mind and heart, as the excerpt below illustrates.

For many months I decided to take a break from reading rock magazines mainly to rest and clear my head from all the folk lore and current affair journalism that had been piling up since weve become a lot of peoples (dare I say) breakfast lunch and dinner gossip. Last month I thought Id take a peek at a few rock mags to see if things have cooled down. Well, to my estimation many trees have been wasted on account of bored and boring people who still like NIRVANA DRECK... We simply wanted to give those dumb heavy metal kids (the kids who we used to be) an introduction to a different way of thinking and some 15 years worth of emotionally and socially important music and all we got was flack, backstabbing and Pearl Jam.

—Kurt Cobain, *Journals*, © 2002 by The End of Music LLCN. Published by Riverhead Books, a member of Penguin Putnam, Inc., with portions reproduced in an excerpt in *Newsweek* titled "If You Read You'll Judge," on Oct. 28, 2002.

Journal writing should help you to reflect not only on your life experiences, but also on what works—or doesn't work—for you. Then, you can explore the next step: the solutions. Here are a few questions you may ask yourself:

- What do you consider your best accomplishment this week?
- How could you further improve upon it?
- What do you consider your least successful accomplishment this week?
- Why do you think you were unable to do better?
- How would you do it differently if you had another chance?

In your journal, raise questions about yourself, issues, and life, and then use the journal to answer them.

JOURNAL WRITING AND JOURNALISM

You'll see in the example below that *journal* and *journalism* are close cousins. In journal entries, writers record what they see, hear, and feel, documenting impressions and opinions about a person or event. Similarly, in journalism, the goal is to report what's happening without relying on feelings.

The following excerpt is taken from a first-person perspective of an American woman of Iraqi descent prior to the 2003 U.S. invasion in Iraq. Her report, which accompanied a larger story about the rise of Saddam Hussein, blends journal-type writing with traditional news reporting techniques. Written in a journalistic style, her writing takes us back to a family gathering that occurred more than 25 years earlier, and it sets the stage for emotional content to follow.

The Baghdad I Knew

It was like a scene from "My Big Fat Greek Wedding," except with Arabs. Dozens of my dark-eyed relations were gathered in my uncle Ibrahim's front yard to celebrate yet another Ali marriage. They skewer-cooked fish, argued politics and kicked a soccer ball around in the 125-degree Baghdad summer heat. It was 1976; I was 11 years old and had never been to Iraq; my dad had immigrated to Los Angeles before I was born. The kids treated my sister and me like novelty items—they couldn't stop fighting over us. My feisty cousin Afrah threw a Sadoon Jaber record onto the ancient player and the girls tried to teach us how to "dance like the Arab." We shook our skinny kid hips, never quite catching the beat. My sister then popped her own Elton John cassette into a clunky tape player we'd lugged all the way from L.A. and shimmied like Cher to "Crocodile Rock." They laughed so hard someone actually spit up a date. That's how I want to remember Baghdad.

Last week President Bush's speech at the United Nations almost guaranteed that my country, America, will soon be engaged in a battle with Iraq, my ancestral homeland. Military analysts on the evening news are already speaking of bombarding Baghdad first for a "strategic edge." Never mind that the densely populated city is home to 5 million people (about 100 of whom I am related to), or that my cousin Zaniab or her baby or my uncle Hassan are far more likely to be taken out than Saddam himself. To be an Iraqi-American right now means to be on edge, to cry a lot, not to sleep at night. I need to hold on to those sweet and simple images.

Believe me, I would like nothing more than to see Saddam's regime fall, but I do not want the Iraqi people crushed under the rubble—again. As concerned as I am about smart bombs' going stupidly awry, I also worry that in a crisis, Saddam will turn on his own countrymen as he's done in the past. There are more than 400,000 Iraqi-Americans, most of whom live in Detroit, Chicago, New York and Los Angeles. Without exception, every one I've talked with—in fact, every Arab-American—wants Saddam out. "I don't think any Iraqi is really sorry that he is going to go," says Hassan

> Fattah, 31, an American-born journalist of Iraqi descent. "The issue is, at what cost?" We are facing a deadly drama in which there are no perfect alternatives...
>
> —Lorraine Ali, *Newsweek*, September 23, 2002

You likely found the style here easy to follow. The opening anecdote, with a clever reference to one of the year's top-grossing movies, draws us into the human scale of the story. The author's personal observations become a photograph for us: We see what she sees.

From time to time, reread your journal entries to see if additional stories and facts can be added. Journalists have numerous stories in their journals still waiting to be written. For now, they're just sketches of their thoughts. You, too, will have such stories once you begin to write on a regular basis. Use your journal for reflection, and for growth as an individual and as a writer.

Section IV

JOURNALISM

CHAPTER SEVENTEEN

Writing a News Story

Readers have certain expectations when looking at a news story, and writers are wise to keep them in mind. The expectations can best be summed up in three questions:

1. What is the news?
2. Why should I care?
3. Is the information accurate and fair?

A story that addresses these concerns promptly and clearly is likely to be read. Question 1, What is the news, is something readers will want to know right away so it must be pointed out clearly at the beginning of the story.

Question 2, Why should I care, may sound callous, but it is ultimately the driving concern that makes people chose one story over the thousands of others they could be reading.

As for question 3, a news story should be an accurate and balanced account of events, taking note of contradictory opinion and pointing out the available evidence.

STRUCTURE OF A NEWS STORY

News stories can be approached in many different ways. A straightforward approach—getting directly to the facts—works best when the news is especially fresh or urgent. A light, humorous tone may also work well with appropriate subject matter. And an anecdote can personalize and introduce a story that readers might otherwise have trouble relating to.

As with all forms of writing, it's essential to consider your audience, and what it likely knows already about the subject of your article. The composition of your audience will affect the structure of your article. Local newspapers, for example, will run stories that people have not heard about elsewhere—the results of a town meeting, the details of a car accident, or the score of a high-school basketball game. Such stories will usually have the facts at the beginning, with no need for an introduction.

In *Newsweek*'s case, the magazine can safely assume that its readers are already aware of major national-news stories—they've heard about them from more immediate media sources. What readers expect from *Newsweek* is a story that makes sense of the issues and adds perspective. In order to accomplish this goal, *Newsweek* stories often begin with an introduction that illustrates the story's significance.

No matter what device you use to get into the story—scene-setting, anecdote, or action lead—you should specify very quickly the major news event or development that has just occurred. Logic might suggest that the background come first, since the past both preceded and produced the current events, but the goal here is to give the reader the freshest, "newsiest" material first.

Newspaper stories are usually written in the "inverted pyramid" format, with the most important information at the start of the story (the lead), and the remaining facts included in order of descending importance. Articles are written this way so that if the reader stops midway through the article, she can be assured of having gotten the most important information. Since they are frequently cut, newspaper articles rarely have formal conclusions.

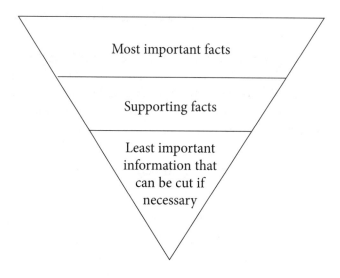

Most important facts

Supporting facts

Least important information that can be cut if necessary

Newsmagazine articles often take a more literary approach. That's because there is more room to write and because they can "afford" to (readers are likely to read the entire piece). The magazine lead is similar to a newspaper lead in that it draws the reader into the story; it typically does this, however, by setting up the story with an anecdote or chronological introduction, not by revealing the most important information the way a newspaper story does. After the lead comes the billboard, which is the article's main idea. The article's body provides supporting details and arguments, and as in an essay, has self-contained paragraphs.

> ### WRITING TEACHES LOGICAL THINKING
>
> "Writing teaches logical thinking and the sequencing of ideas. It's the best way to learn how to tell a story, even if you're planning to tell that story in images and sounds and hyperlinks. And the only way to learn how to write is to write—a lot."
>
> —Michael Rogers, General Manager of Newsweek.com, 2000

The conclusion of a magazine news article is called a *kicker*. Rather than summarizing or formally concluding the article, the kicker leaves readers with something to think about. Regardless of how they feel about the topic, they're left to consider the future ramifications of what has been discussed.

Structure of a Newsmagazine Article

LEAD
BILLBOARD
DEVELOPMENT
(A) main idea and supporting details
(B) main idea and supporting details
(C) main idea and supporting details
KICKER

You should note that although this is the most common format for a story, it isn't required all of the time. Beyond the standard structure, there are some essentials that every piece of journalistic writing should have. We trust those in the media to get the story right, to check their facts, and to cover the news objectively. All stories should be:

- Accurate
- Fair
- Clear
- Appropriate for their length

ACCURACY AND FAIRNESS

It is difficult to write about one of these subjects without writing about the other. They are closely connected. When a story is inaccurate, there can be many negative consequences: A longtime reader may be offended or readers' faith in journalists may be compromised. But also, there could be lawsuits, loss of jobs, and damage to people or organizations' reputations.

Facts should come from authoritative sources: the police, government officials, public documents (such as budgets), and open public meetings. Eyewitness accounts to any major event should be included. Wherever possible, the writer should be an eyewitness to the topic—by attending a hearing, researching public documents, or visiting a facility.

Double check all the facts in your story. And if you are less than 100 percent certain about anything, call your source back and ask for clarification of what was discussed. He'll appreciate this call much more than an apologetic call after the story has appeared with erroneous information attributed to him!

- Double-check the spelling of all proper names, no matter how simple they appear. Make sure that *Jane* isn't actually spelled *Jayne*. Also, someone you have been calling by the name of *Rudy* may actually prefer to be addressed by his full name, *Rodolfo*, in print.

- Visit any websites you cite to make sure you've provided the correct address (copy and paste the address into your document and recheck it to be certain you've written it correctly).

- Personally call any phone numbers your story includes to make sure that they're accurate and that the person on the other end of the phone is ready to receive the calls that will inevitably follow the publication of your story.

- Make certain that any quotations used in the story are the exact words that were spoken. If you're unsure about whether they were, don't use the quote. In that case, paraphrase the quote (restate the original idea in your own words). A source who is misquoted may be less likely to grant another interview in the future. No writer would want to hear these words from a valued source: "Why should I talk to you? You'll only mess it up anyway."

- Make sure your quotes are presented in context. A writer has a great responsibility to not only quote interview subjects accurately, but also in the context in which the statements were intended. Nothing can rile an interview subject more than when an unusual, off-hand comment is isolated from a lengthy interview and sensationalized. If you quote the basketball coach saying, "I'm glad we lost," you would be seriously remiss to present that quote alone to readers if the coach had in fact continued to say, "Since it was the last regular-season game and meaningless in terms of our seeding in the playoffs, our players have a clear understanding of how lousy it feels to lose. I'm now more confident than ever that we'll keep winning until we capture the title."

Being accurate means giving the whole story—not just the story that's immediately apparent. It helps to keep in mind that rarely is anyone "100 percent right." All sources, whether intentionally or not, are likely to avoid saying things that cast them in a bad light, so you must aggressively look elsewhere for evidence to the contrary.

Any story written about a controversial topic—no matter how small the controversy—should be balanced. Balanced reporting occurs when all sides, arguments, and opinions are presented, and when all parties are given an opportunity to share information. Though it is impossible to completely eliminate your own bias from a story, try your best to ensure that it's kept to a minimum.

So, just how do you analyze a news story for objectivity?

1. Compare headlines and story content. How accurately does the actual headline encapsulate the article? Does the headline slant one's reading of the article?

2. Identify politically charged labels, adjectives, and verbs. Word choices can help identify reporters' biases.

3. Question the hidden agenda of suspicious sources and try to identify whose view has been left out. Unnamed sources sometimes use their anonymity to further their own agendas.

4. Consider whether the placement of ideas and sources affects story impact. Whose position is stressed by the arrangement of the story?

5. Look for diverse perspectives. How does the news change when seen from the perspectives of people of both genders and different races and beliefs?

6. Compare photographs and photo captions to the news stories connected with them to see if they are faithful to the related articles.

7. Compare news stories to common sense.

8. Question polling data and statistics to see if they are presented to support a certain perspective.

CLARITY

The best writing is simple, clear, and free of clutter. If it isn't, your reader is sure to lose interest.

- Use dynamic verbs.
- Avoid abstractions; explain anything that is unclear.
- Stick to the facts—and avoid inserting opinion.
- Describe the people, places, and things that are essential to the story.

- Steer clear of clichés (overused phrases such as *clean as a whistle*) and jargon (words such as *perpetrators* or *collateral damage* that are typically used only by professionals in a given field).
- Stay away from hearsay. Hearsay involves second-hand news—accounts that sound first-hand but in fact are made by people who did not actually witness an event. Such statements can be confusing and invite skepticism: "Who is this person, and why didn't the reporter go straight to the source?" a reader would want to know.

The term *hearsay* is often used in court settings, where hearsay testimony is rarely allowed ("I testify that Jones told me that Smith confessed to the crime"). If you have no choice but to use hearsay in a story, be sure it is clear to your reader why you are doing so.

FIRST-HAND SOURCES ONLY

In reporting, steer clear of sources who did not experience the topic first-hand. They can be used as a stepping stone—to lead you to the actual source—but do not build your case around second-hand sources. After all, would you listen to a person who said, "France is a great place, though I've never been there"?

The following essay succeeds as a news story in several ways. It has a cohesive structure: a lead, a billboard statement ("Bechler's death has reignited an intense debate"), development in the form of supporting evidence about the product's appeal and possibilities of misuse, and a kicker that suggests it might be best to steer clear of supplements.

Are We Dying to Be Thin?

The makers of the wildly popular rapid weight-loss supplement Xenadrine RFA-1 like to brag in ads that their product "makes national news." Last week's headlines can't have been what they had in mind. Baltimore Orioles pitcher Steve Bechler died in Florida after heatstroke drove his temperature to 108 degrees. Struggling to lose weight, the 23-year-old had been taking Xenadrine RFA-1, according to Orioles officials. Broward County medical examiner Joshua Perper put the ephedra-packed pill at the top of his list of possible factors in Bechler's death.

Shane Freedman, general counsel for Xenadrine's manufacturer, Cytodyne Technologies, calls the link "extremely premature and bordering on reckless." But for years, watchdog groups and physicians have been saying the same thing about the hype surrounding ephedra. Bechler's death has reignited an intense debate about the safety of the herb, one that began almost as soon as its popularity mushroomed thanks to aggressive advertising in 1994—the same year that the FDA lost power to regulate dietary supplements. Since then, more than 1,400 adverse reactions and 100 deaths have been blamed on ephedra-based supplements—and some 12 million dieters and athletes want to know if they are at risk.

There's little doubt about ephedra's popularity. The herb is found in all four of America's best-selling weight-loss products—which together generate more than $161 million in annual sales—and is a hit with athletes, particularly bodybuilders, despite being banned by many sports leagues (but not Major League Baseball). Athletes are especially prone to ephedra abuse, notes nutritionist Rehan Jalali, head of the Supplement Research Foundation, a fitness-information center. Teens are more likely to ignore guidelines and overuse the products, too. Since most ephedra pills aren't meant for kids under 18, health stores like GNC have recently started carding potential buyers. Minors can still get their hands on ephedra, though. The cheap Yellow Jackets brand was a favorite of 16-year-old Illinois football player Sean Riggins. He died last year; the coroner blamed an ephedra-induced heart attack. The brand is now banned, but others still crowd shelves.

Athletes and teens aren't the only ones taking chances. Though healthy users who take recommended doses are probably safe, many doctors say the herb poses a serious risk for patients with hypertension, heart disease, overactive thyroids, or diabetes. Bechler belonged to the first group. His high blood pressure, combined with rapid weight loss, may have weakened his body—already strained by ephedra and workouts in the Florida heat.

Ephedra's potential danger is a function of its active ingredient, ephedrine, which stimulates beta receptors on fat cells. This increases metabolism, causing the body to burn more fat. Heart cells also carry beta receptors. When combined with caffeine—as it almost always is in supplements—ephedrine stimulates those cells, too, raising the heart rate and blood pressure and sometimes causing insomnia, an irregular heartbeat or even a heart attack or stroke.

Bad publicity, skyrocketing insurance rates and GNC's carding policy have convinced many makers to pull their ephedra products and introduce new alternatives in the past few months. All are heavy on caffeine; some also contain substances similar to ephedra, like bitter orange and octopamine. The new products may be safer than ephedra, and anyone can buy them, but they're largely untested and their huge caffeine loads aren't heart-healthy. Jalali, who sometimes uses ephedra, is switching to several new substitutes. You could do the same. But there's only one sure way to avoid risk: don't take weight-loss supplements at all.

—Mary Carmichael, *Newsweek*, March 3, 2003

Think, for a moment, about the length of this story—fewer than 600 words. Quite possibly, this could be a *Newsweek* cover story. A writer would easily have been able to write a longer piece about this subject. Yet in the space of less than one magazine page, it provides us with a great deal of information. How? It sticks to the framework of a magazine article yet includes not a single irrelevant sentence. Additionally:

- The story cites authoritative sources such as the Broward County coroner and the head of the Supplement Research Foundation.

- Scientific explanations provide support for theory that the weight-loss supplement might be dangerous.
- A lawyer for the supplement's manufacturer is invited to give comment, providing the viewpoint of the other side.
- The article explains in plain English how ephedra works. A less talented writer likely would have struggled to assemble that explanation.
- "Are We Dying to be Thin?" is a perfect headline here, as it points up the main debate. An awful headline would have been "Drug Kills Baseball Star." Why? For starters, ephedrine is an herb, not a drug—an important distinction. Also, ephedrine wasn't confirmed as the cause of death, merely noted as a possible cause. Retractions would have been demanded for such errors. Lastly, the headline would not be truly accurate because the story does not focus on the death of the baseball player—it focuses on the debate about the drug.

WRITING TO A SPECIFIC LENGTH

Your editor or instructor should give you an assigned length for your stories. If a teacher vaguely tells you to write "until you're done" without giving you a measurement, she's testing your news judgment. In that case, be ready to write at least a two-page story that thoroughly addresses the subject matter.

Once you know how much you're supposed to write, you know what you have to do. Newspaper writers have it a bit easier here; they stick to the *inverted pyramid* format that emphasizes placement of the most important facts first. A short news story might be six paragraphs with one or two sentences each. It would lead with the facts, limiting background and quotations to no more than a paragraph or two.

Magazine writers must be more creative. In their case, "shorter" doesn't necessarily mean abandoning the lead-billboard-development-kicker approach. It does mean tightening up each aspect and being especially mindful of the need for every word to advance the article's main idea.

> **HEADLINE CAPTURES STORY!**
>
> At its best, a headline captures the essence of a story. At its worst, it sensationalizes one out-of-context detail of a story without paying attention to the actual facts.

DEVELOPING YOUR NEWS STORY

As is the case when writing an essay, you might have a hard time picking a topic. First, brainstorm ideas about timely issues that interest you. Then, consider whether your ideas are indeed newsworthy. Would others be interested in reading a news piece about these topics? Your topics may have to do with national or international politics, a new policy at your school, or a controversy in your community.

To help you select one topic out of this group of ideas, take the following steps. Ultimately, you'll want to choose the topic for which you have the strongest case. You should have a good sense of this once you have completed step 1.

Step 1: Identify what you already know about the topic.

Make a list or web to record what you already know. You'll also need to know "what you don't know." That is, as a journalist, you'll need to know what questions need to be answered in order to make this a thorough piece of writing. It will also be necessary to figure out precisely how and where you'll be able to get information that will answer those questions.

The model below might help. In one column, write what you know. In the next column, write what you need to find out. In the last column, write whom you will need to ask or what resources you will need to answer the question. Let's follow an example:

What I know:	What do I need to find out?	How will I find out?
The town council has proposed a building in town—a casino—right off the highway.	Who will decide whether to pass the proposal?	Talk to the head of the town council
	What do people in the community think of the proposal?	Interview people to see what they think
	Have any groups or people organized to express their opinion? What are their opinions?	Identify the groups and their leaders and ask them for their viewpoint
	What effects would the casino have on the community?	Ask those who proposed the casino; those who oppose the project; and members of citizens' groups on both sides of the issue

Step 2. Gather and organize your data.

Now it's time to start the groundwork: Make phone calls, send email, set up interviews, plan visits, and gather information from sources. Once you have pulled together substantial information, you'll need it organized. There are several ways to organize data. You can:

- Put each piece of information on an index card and sort the cards into piles, according to topic.
- Color-code your notes, with each color identifying information that supports a particular point.
- Create a web, with the center stating the issue and each branch listing a question.
- Create lists in your word-processing program. Pose a question at the top of each list and place the answers underneath.

Step 3. Organize the presentation of the news story.

Use a formula to define sections of your article, including what each section will do and what you will include in it.

Part I: What is its function?
What are the main points?

Part II: What is its function?
What are the main points?

Part III: What is its function?
What are the main points?

Step 4. Write your news story.

Be sure to share it with a peer to get feedback and ideas for improvement. Revise as necessary.

CHAPTER EIGHTEEN

Writing a Feature Story

Unlike a news story, which encapsulates a current event, a feature story takes an in-depth look at an issue—current or not. Usually focused on human interest, it goes behind the scenes at the history and development of a situation. Though not a hard-news piece, a feature usually contains news—just news of a different variety.

The feature writer has a great deal more latitude and time with which to explore a subject than does the news journalist. With fewer severe restrictions on time, more "writerly" techniques can be used, and description, extended quotations, narration, supposition, and interpretation are the norm. Digression—practically forbidden in a typical news story—is allowed, even encouraged, here, and the direction of the story is often left open. Not always focused on one event, features may address patterns of events from which a theory can develop. Some broad subject areas include:

- Human-interest stories
- How-to articles
- Seasonal themes
- Historical facts
- A glimpse of what happens behind the scenes
- Personality profiles

There's actually more to features than just writing. Strong features, including profiles and reviews, demand thorough reporting as well. And while a feature can take a lighter approach to a subject, it doesn't necessarily do so. Features cover the before and after of news, looking at how situations evolve.

NO PERSONAL OPINIONS WANTED

A feature piece is not an opinion piece. It's just a more elaborate, in-depth look at a newsworthy person or issue.

A feature isn't quite as tied to an event as a news story is, but this doesn't mean the feature writer can be sloppier with facts. Quite the contrary. Since features have more potential than hard-news stories to be "fluffy," it's important that feature writers keep a rein on their poetic impulses.

A good feature story:

- Has something compelling about it
- Provides background information
- Reveals a thorough understanding of the issues
- Incorporates interviews and research

STRUCTURE OF A FEATURE STORY

It is common to see features in newsmagazines. *Newsweek,* for instance, frequently includes them on the cover. Except when compelling news events dictate otherwise, the magazine always includes a lively mixture of hard-news stories (recent or dramatic occurrences), softer news (of less immediacy and importance), and features.

With respect to format and topic, there is no set format. Feature writing provides many options—sometimes too many—and that's precisely what can make it challenging. When you have a choice of writing a profile, column, interview, review, ongoing investigation, or exploration of trends, there are few limitations.

At the same time, with so many possible angles, narrowing down a topic can be a daunting task. If you want to write a profile of a certain filmmaker, you might discuss his work in the context of a trend in the arts. If you want to write about an historical event, you might tell it chronologically with background information interspersed, though you might want to start in the middle and flash back to previous events. If you want to write a background story on a current news event, you might look through the eyes of one family in order to make it more personalized.

In the *Associated Press Guide to News Writing*, Rene J. Cappon offers some wisdom on feature-writing:

> Because features are less shackled to the moment than hard-news stories, writers usually have more time. Proper use of that time takes a special discipline. Some writers, unfortunately, use it to land their copy with clusters of adjectives, purple passages and other decorative devices. If you feel the decorative impulse coming on, lie down until it goes away. Strong feature writing is simple, clear, orderly, free of labored mannerisms and tricks that call attention to the writing itself rather than the substance.
>
> … The news story starts from an event. The feature story starts from an idea. 'Let's do a story on the changes in Appalachia,' the editor decides. 'There haven't been any changes,' the reporter discovers. 'Fine, then let's do a story on why not. After all, the government poured millions into the place.'
>
> This is vague, but that's how it should be. Redefining and massaging the idea is the outcome of, not the preliminary to, reporting. Neither you nor your editor can know in advance where the scent will lead you …

INTERVIEWING

Interviewing is an integral part of writing a feature. In fact, it is your primary method of obtaining information. When we have a question that we cannot answer by ourselves or by looking in a book, we seek out an expert. Similarly, journalists interview those who are famous or expert in their field.

An expert provides a deeper perspective of the story at hand. Oftentimes, in agreeing to be interviewed on a subject, the expert has no hidden agenda behind offering his expertise. However, it is possible—and sometimes indeed the case—that an expert who provides his educated opinion surrounding the given circumstances proactively wants certain information to reach the public. That is why he agrees to the discussion in the first place.

EXPECT SOME LONG PAUSES

While interviewing an expert is often a smooth process, it can also get tricky: Even experts at times will not want to respond to certain questions because they'll have to commit to a response that others won't like.

Sometimes, however, journalists interview people who are neither famous nor expert, but who lead interesting lives; they might have an unusual occupation, family, hobby, or living situation. These people, the everyday "Joe," often provide information that piques our interest even more than the opinions of the famous. We can relate to them more than we can to movie stars and international leaders. In an interview, we can learn about how a person started out and what decisions she made that led to a particularly public—or quiet—life. If we can think of the right questions and create the right atmosphere, many interviews can produce interesting "copy" or material.

In order to create a balanced feature story, interview at least three sources for information. These sources should be first-hand sources; that is, people who had direct contact with the topic at hand. You may be asked to provide questions ahead of time to some interviewees so that they can prepare the answers.

Giving the interviewee an idea of the questions ahead of time may make him more comfortable and forthright, though chances are, you'll eliminate the element of surprise. At other times, it's more effective to ask questions on the spot, in order to get a gut reaction or an honest response. When you're interviewing someone about a controversial issue, you'll want to take this approach, where the questions are not provided ahead of time—that is, unless the interviewee stipulates beforehand that you do otherwise.

We have all seen interviews where the person is uncomfortable or distressed. They can be painful to watch. On the whole, if someone agrees to be interviewed, do your best to make the person feel comfortable. You're more likely to get thorough and spontaneous answers—even when asking difficult questions.

You'll also need to think on your feet. Your interviewee may go off on a tangent that's more interesting than your original topic. Be ready to go there. If you need to return to your original question after you've veered off-course, you'll have to be assertive and guide your interviewee back on course. Of course if the interview is intended as a profile or an informal interview, letting the person digress may turn out to be a positive. Some of the most worthwhile and compelling interviews have been the result of spontaneous talk.

What questions should you ask? That's up to you, of course, but there should be a mixture of those that allow the subject some leeway and those that probe a specific point. If you are interviewing a local elected official, you might first ask, "What are your goals for the current term?" and then follow-up with, "Why did you vote for a tax increase when the county doesn't face a budget shortfall this year?" If you ask only questions of the first variety, you are going "too easy" on your subject, allowing him to dictate the entire agenda.

If you ask only questions of the second variety, you will come across as predatory—seeking only to expose weaknesses. In such cases, the subject may recoil and give limited responses. Who, after all, would want to be interviewed by someone who has the singular mission to show that you're ineffective?

As you might expect, this balancing act isn't always easy to maintain, but it is an important thing to have. Any subject worth interviewing deserves the chance to answer open-ended questions in addition to those questions that are more challenging. Don't feel guilty about asking tough questions—serious topics demand them!

When interviewing, remember:

- Anyone who grants you an interview should be treated with respect.
- Select a location where your interviewee is comfortable (if asking questions about a controversial subject, this may not be possible or even preferable—or, you may not have a choice).
- Do your homework—research the interviewee's background and opinions. (In other words, if you're interviewing a banker, don't ask for the definition of a stock or bond.)
- Do not ask basic or yes/no questions. Interviewees are impressed by questions that they have to think about.
- Ask several types of questions: open-ended, challenging, general, and specific.

Following is a feature story on a bright newcomer in the fashion world. As you read, make a list of questions you think the author may have asked herself before writing this piece.

Fashion's Freshman Face

Like a lot of high-school boys, Esteban Cortazar keeps pictures of pretty girls in his notebook. But unlike most, the 18-year-old junior at Miami's Design and Architecture Senior High moons over Giselle and J. Lo because he dreams of dressing, not undressing, them. Custom Garment Making 4 is his favorite class, and today he shows his teacher, Ms. Pringle, Polaroid shots of his spring collection. She lays out the photos of the flowing electric-aqua and yellow silk designs before her and pronounces them beautiful. Might there be a seat for her at the show if she can get the day off? she asks. Cortazar is thrilled. He says he will take care of it.

This week Esteban Cortazar will unveil his collection at Fashion Week in New York, the youngest designer to debut there. Is he a great talent? It's hard to say, since no one but Ms. Pringle has yet seen more than 20 of his flirty, feminine pieces. Can he make it in the rough-and-tumble fashion world? Too soon to tell, but already the industry is salivating. The New York *Times* has heralded his arrival. And Saks sees much promise. "He was all giggly, and that was rubbing off on us. You wanted to dive into the rack," says Saks' Michael Fink of the sneak preview he got recently. As for Cortazar, he went down a red carpet at a party this summer and can't wait to do it again. "It's such a cool feeling because I've always loved attention. And I knew how to handle it because I like it. I love it."

Born in Bogota, Cortazar used to admire the fancy dresses his mother wore when she sang at jazz clubs. At 10, Cortazar moved in with his dad (his parents separated when he was a year old), a painter, who lived above News Cafe in South Beach, where Gianni Versace famously read his morning paper. "We were living in a very beautiful way," says his father, Valentino. "He would always bring me his friends for me to paint."

As South Beach came into its own in the early '90s, so did Cortazar. At 13 he started dressing windows at his local vintage-clothing store. That same year he did his first collection for the sixth-grade talent show. He trained three girlfriends how to walk— "Show me Naomi!" he'd command. Inspiration was right out his window. "I watched Claudia Schiffer being photographed by Patrick Demarchelier in front of my building. Just fabulous," says Cortazar.

He understood the necessary art of self-promotion at a young age, and introduced himself to Madonna, Versace and Todd Oldham, who took his young fan to Fashion Week in New York when he was 13. A year later Cortazar charmed Ferdinand Grandi, who would eventually agree to bankroll the designer based on about 20 colored-pencil sketches. When Kal Ruttenstein of Bloomingdale's was in Miami earlier this year, Cortazar took a model with him over to the trendmaker's room at the Delano for a private showing of the mini fall collection. Ruttenstein liked the feathered and ruffled gowns, which Cortazar describes as "Betty Boop in Sevilla," enough to put them in his New York City windows.

Though he's been preparing for years, Cortazar's now scrambling. No. 1 on his "to do" list is to get a pearl-stitch machine. No. 11 is "ask Alison for Algebra homework." "I can't believe it. I'm so excited! This is crazy. Wow wow wow wow." The fashionistas couldn't have said it better themselves.

—Susannah Meadows, *Newsweek*, September 23, 2002

The author may have asked herself the following questions before writing this story:

- Who is Esteban Cortazar and what kinds of challenges has he had?
- Why is he so popular at the moment?
- What is his appeal? Has he introduced any new trends or styles?
- Where can consumers buy his clothes?

This feature succeeds on several levels. It focuses on a unique subject—something we don't hear about every day. In addition to vividly describing the designs, the text includes lively quotes that capture the designer's enthusiasm. Mostly, the writing is fresh and the topic is timely, as the designer is about to debut his collection.

DEVELOPING YOUR FEATURE STORY

To select your topic, observe your surroundings and your world. Consider the following questions:

- Is someone you know particularly interesting, worthy of a profile?

- Do you have a unique perspective on a topic that's already been discussed?

- Do you notice a trend somewhere—a change in the way people are dressing, socializing, driving, or eating?

- Is there a situation (applying for college tuition aid, teenage pregnancy) that merits a closer look?

- Is there a feature story to be found within a hard-news story? Was something unexplained?

- Do you know of a large institution, employer, or organization you think deserves higher visibility?

- What are people doing with their free time?

Make inquiries about everything around you for possible storylines. Be sure to jot down notes to help you recall your ideas later on. Then you'll need to select three people related to the topic whom you'd like to interview.

CHAPTER NINETEEN

Writing a Letter to the Editor

Because so much of our mass media is one-way, it isn't often that people get to provide feedback on what they see and hear. Too often, people's own responses to issues in the media go unheard. An editorial letter is a way around that. It's an exciting feeling to see your letter in the local newspaper or in a news magazine—and for most of us, it's the closest we get to being published.

Why write a letter to the editor?

- To show that you care about what's happening in your community or the world
- To show that you're a careful reader of the publication
- To express disagreement with the substance or tone of an article
- To offer support or praise for an article
- To exercise your ability to analyze the news and its presentation
- To hone your talents in crafting a concise, cogent argument
- To show others (including, possibly, prospective employers and colleges) that you have the intellect and the enthusiasm about news to take a stand

Letters to the editor can take different forms. The most popular type, of course, is the traditional feedback letter to a newspaper or journal; that is, a brief letter expressing your feelings about a particular issue, news story, or column. Editorial letters can also take the form of an opinion column or a political cartoon.

STRUCTURE OF AN EDITORIAL LETTER

What criteria do editors use to screen the hundreds of letters they receive each week? Why should your letter be chosen for printing above all of the others? The answer to this question can be summed up in two words: concise and descriptive.

If it does one thing well, a letter to the editor should present one argument concisely. No one is interested in reading a rambling treatise on an article's merits and faults.

> **ACT QUICKLY**
>
> If you read an article to which you feel the need to respond, send off your letter right away. By waiting more than a week, you run the risk of not having it printed.

The topic of an editorial letter is highly focused: It responds to a specific article of interest. In addition, it:

- Expresses your interpretation of the article
- Explains your opinion about the issue
- Introduces a perspective that was not explored in the original article

MAKE YOUR POINT UP TOP

Editors do cut letters deemed too long for printing, so make sure you've made your point up top. There's a limited amount of space, so don't be surprised if your letter appears in abbreviated form.

Let's look at some examples. These are a few letters that *Newsweek* received in response to articles on the topic of whether television is good for kids.

Letter 1

As a stay-at-home mother of two, I must concur with Daniel McGinn ("Guilt Free TV," Nov. 11). I, too, have been pleasantly surprised by the caliber and quantity of programs for preschoolers. I find my children's favorite shows to be an ally in reinforcing messages I teach at home. How can I fault programs demonstrating manners, problem-solving and tolerance? Children learn through example. Relating my son's experience on a playdate to Clifford and his friends speaks volumes over my parental lectures on sharing.

—Marie Hines, Grayslake, Illinois
(Reprinted with Permission)

Letter 2

Karen Springen says that her kids don't "watch TV. Period. Not at home, not at friends' houses" ("Why We Tuned Out"). What planet does she live on? If her kids don't watch TV at friends' houses now, they certainly will later, and without telling her. My 11-year-old son's classmates tell me what their parents don't allow them to watch, but they do anyway. I let my son watch TV because I watch it with him. He doesn't think it's cool or rebellious because, unlike his repressed classmates, he doesn't associate it with getting away with anything. I should add that my son is fit, physically active and a gifted student. Maybe it is Springen who has decided to tune out—the world.

—Karen Worden, Lancaster, California
(Reprinted with Permission)

Letter 3

It is disheartening that Daniel McGinn has not only misled himself in his quest to be a better-informed parent, but has used *Newsweek* to mislead other parents. As an educator for 15 years and a parent of two children, I have to disagree with his premise that "parents are recognizing that television can be beneficial." Or are parents like McGinn just condoning a habit that they themselves cannot break? While parents permit children to watch, two important phenomena occur: the habit of television viewing (in place of other activities such as reading) is being formed, and the messages of commercial TV (Watch more! Buy products!) are being absorbed. In the words of Groucho Marx, "I find television very educating. Every time somebody turns on the set, I go into the other room and read a book."

—Theresa A. Deckebach, Reading Specialist,
Wissahickon School District, Glenside, PA
(Reprinted with Permission)

Letter 4

Your cover story presents a conundrum. At first I was amazed at the discrepancy in the length of the pieces. The argument in favor of children's television is much longer than the essay that advances the idea of going without. But I realize the glass is half full. TV is well documented as being a catalyst for fostering a short attention span. Perhaps your readers won't finish reading the longer pro-TV argument and flip past it, but they might well make it through the piece that skillfully questions TV's necessity. In any event, the eternal television problem is that kids aren't just watching what's made for them. It's the rest of the programming we should be concerned about—and turn off.

—Erika Tarlin, Somerville, Massachusetts
(Reprinted with Permission)

All of these letters express different viewpoints on the same issue. Letter 1 supports the article's findings and uses a personal example to illuminate her point. Letter 2 suggests forcefully that Karen Springen may be misguided in her efforts to shield her kids from TV, again citing a personal experience. Letter 3 reasonably challenges the foundations of the pro-TV crowd, and incorporates an amusing yet poignant quote from Groucho Marx. And letter 4 uses a more creative approach to poke fun at the pro-TV movement, questioning the magazine's allotment of space to the "anti-TV" article.

The letters above are enjoyable to read because they:

- Attempt to make only one point
- Are brief, which encourages readers to take a look
- Rely on logic and personal experience to support their ideas
- Are clearly written

You cannot possibly agree with all four letter writers, since they express divergent views, but you can still find them all engaging and interesting. This is the beauty of the letters page of a publication: It serves as a vigorous forum for the expression of all viewpoints, even those you don't agree with. Those who feel strongly about an issue shouldn't mind reading the convictions of those on the other side—they'll know what logic they're up against when making their case in the future.

DEVELOPING YOUR LETTER TO THE EDITOR

First, decide upon your topic. That's usually quite simple, since you're responding to a specific column or article. You probably have a complaint or wish to express another viewpoint.

Now, you have to clarify your complaint or viewpoint. Focus on one or two points. The less relevant items will only cloud the issue, so if they're not essential to your argument, leave them out. You'll make a stronger case that way.

DON'T SOUND OUTDATED

Make sure your letter is timely. It doesn't have to be about the most current news, but it should be on something of current interest to people.

Next, how are you going to state your case? Of course you're going to state what you believe, but then you need to back it up. Are you going to correct the original article with an opposing fact or statistic? Are you going to include a personal experience? The challenge here is to make your argument concise yet descriptive. Don't forget to write in context of the original article. After all, that's what you're responding to.

While your letter should be brief, make sure you find out the preferred style and format of the news outlet to which you are writing. Some news sources will accept two paragraphs, others a full page. And finally, don't forget to include your name, phone, and email. Chances are that without identifying information, your letter won't even be considered for publishing.

Before you sign off:

- Don't forget to name the article you're writing about. Also, state its publication date in parentheses.
- Make sure your letter is concise. Shoot for 150 words or so. If it's longer than that, chances are it will get cut down at the editor's discretion, and you'll have no way of knowing which part he will cut.

EXPRESS YOUR VIEWS IN OTHER WAYS

Apart from the editorial letter, there are other ways to practice your argumentation skills. Developing these will serve you well after high school.

- Write to your local officials
- Advocate for a cause, such as the environment or healthcare
- Write a letter of complaint to a business or an organization
- Write a column in a student newsletter

CHAPTER TWENTY

Writing a Review

Throughout this book, it has been emphasized that strong writing can help influence decisions and be a force to change minds. This final chapter shows how a well-crafted essay can effect change at the most basic level: by influencing people's decisions on what books to read, what movies to see, and what music to listen to, among other things. Reviews provide practical information and guidance about everyday decisions, making it easier for us to select among countless options.

Why write a review? For starters, you'll always have an audience. Reviews are among the most popular forms of writing because readers appreciate the guidance. If you read that a new restaurant is awful—that the burger was burned to a crisp, the bun was stale, the french fries were soggy, and the service was snobbish—you'd appreciate this information before you learned the hard way! That's how readers of reviews feel, and it explains why reviews are always such a popular item.

Another good reason to write a review is that it's a way for young journalists to get published. As student newspapers and community publications are always in need of quality copy, they are often pleased to run intelligent reviews. If you are trying to get your words published for the first time, this is a good venue for doing so.

DON'T GIVE IT ALL AWAY

If you are writing a book or movie review, don't give away the ending! You'll kill the reader's interest if you divulge the entire plot. Keep an element of suspense.

Writing a review is a terrific way to help you sharpen your writing skills. Not only will it force you to clarify how you feel about something, it will force you to go the next step and convince others of that view in writing. You can review just about anything—a new CD, the latest hamburger creation from your favorite fast-food chain, or an upgrade to a popular computer program. It doesn't matter what it is, as long as you practice.

STRUCTURE OF A REVIEW

A review is a critical analysis of something. Its purpose is neither to restate details nor to state unequivocally that something is awful or fantastic. Your opinion should come through, yes, but with details and description explaining what prompted you to feel this way. It isn't enough to just state your opinion; you must explain why you feel the way you do.

A review provides a concise summary of the plot. You want to describe to some degree the setting and scene. At the basic level, you need to give the reader some background about the story, as well as provide context for what you are about to say. Also important is the intention the author or filmmaker had for writing the book or making the movie. Naturally, this isn't always apparent, but you should do your best to objectively figure this out. After all, since your goal is to determine whether the work is successful at what it set out to do, you have to first know the initial purpose on the part of the creator.

A review is reasonably brief. Reviews are not intended to be long essays. They're usually a few paragraphs in length and concise. This is not the place to go on and on about details. Pick a few things you liked or didn't like about the work and stop there.

The language of a review is relaxed and conversational. Your writing should be easy to understand, as if you were providing a critique in person. People are seeking your advice as a peer and they expect you to "tell it straight." When we say peer, this has nothing to do with age: We really mean, "as a fellow human being" who might be interested in the subject being reviewed. As easily as your friend would read your review, so too could your grandparent. In fact, anyone reading it should be able to relate to your advice: Language should be formal enough for adults, yet informal enough for a younger reader.

A review is credible and fair. "How can I be fair," you might ask, "if the movie was absolutely awful?" Fairness can be shown by communicating an attempt to at least *try* to find something likeable about the movie. Maybe one actor stood out. Maybe the special effects were stunning. When you try to find something positive, you'll come across as more credibile. Additionally, it signals your neutrality when you entered this assignment—that you didn't set out to find fault with the piece. Similarly, when writing a glowing review, it's best to point out at least one shortcoming. Why? Because true perfection is rarely found.

In the course of your evaluation, make sure you consider whether there's another way to look at the presentation. Don't be quick to make an opinion statement until you have convinced yourself that there's no other way to look at it.

Having said that, the tone must have a certain slant either recommending or finding fault with the item at hand. That's because readers ultimately want to know whether to seek out this item.

BOOK REVIEWS

A book review is a personal assessment—a critique—explaining how well an author has covered a specific topic. As a reviewer, you analyze the book for how well it tells a story or conveys information. And more than that, you evaluate the quality of writing and organization. Is it a fresh and creative approach, or has it been said before? Above all, has the book helped in your understanding of the subject at hand?

A REVIEW IS NOT AN OBJECTIVE ESSAY

You want to state your opinion, albeit subtly. Make sure your opinion comes through the entire text. Don't just state it once at the beginning and assume that your readers will remember it.

The book review should also feature an objective description of the storyline, so readers can understand the review's context. You want to make things concrete. Remember, you're writing for people who have not yet read the book, so providing abstract commentary won't be helpful unless some specifics are also included. Feel free to cite direct text and quotations from the book (using quotation marks where needed), but don't go overboard. Just cutting and pasting long quotations from the book will not only bore your reader, it will focus your review too heavily on details.

Yet a book review is not just a retelling of the story. Readers want to know what you think of the book; they also want enough information about the strengths, weaknesses and content to form an opinion of their own.

Before writing your review, remember the basic questions that every news story is supposed to answer: Who? What? When? Where? Why? How? Ask yourself the same questions about the book—and be sure you have a clear understanding of the answers—before you begin to write. Here are some sample questions to consider:

- What type of book is this (fiction, nonfiction, biography, or autobiography)?
- What is the plot? Who are the main characters? When and where does the main action take place?
- How does the story unfold? Why is the story told in this manner?
- What point of view is expressed?
- What are the book's strong and weak points?
- What examples illustrate my overall feelings about the book?
- How strong is the writing?
- How could this work be improved?
- Why does the book succeed or fail?

TITLE AND AUTHOR NEEDED

Your review should include the book's title, author, publisher, and price, as well as a reference to the cover being hard-backed or paper.

Following are some other things to consider when writing a book review. Naturally, these things don't apply to only a book; they can be adapted to any item that's being addressed.

- Is the book interesting, memorable, entertaining or instructive? Why?
- Does the book leave out any important issues?
- Which of the author's opinions do you agree with? disagree with? Why?
- How did the book affect you? Have your opinions about the topic changed?

Let's look at a sample book review that contains a wealth of information—and opinion.

Old Men, Wife-Beaters, Bootleggers—and Brilliance

I f you ride public transportation and read along the way, every book falls into one of two categories: those that make you miss your stop and those that don't. Deep into William Gay's collection of startling Gothic stories, "I Hate to See That Evening Sun Go Down," I missed my stop once and barely made it next time. Unlike so many fiction writers who clobber readers with Meaning, Gay understands that his first responsibility is to tell a good story. And in this book he captivates with bristling tales of old men, bootleggers and wife-beaters in rural Tennessee, where Gay lives. In "The Paperhanger," which was published in *four* anthologies and won an O. Henry Award, a doctor's wife walks out of her house with her 4-year-old in tow, but when the woman reaches her Mercedes her daughter is gone, never to be found. In the final scene, the woman has passed out after sleeping with her wallpaper hanger, one of the many workers at the house the day her child vanished. When she opens her eyes, she'll find out what became of her daughter and, in that thrilling moment—the story ends. In "Those Deep Elm Brown's Ferry Blues," a man with Alzheimer's remembers that he once murdered a townie: "Somewhere on the outskirts of town a siren began, the approaching whoop whoop whoop like some alarm the old man had inadvertently triggered that was homing in on him." In Gay's subtle telling, realizations surface like consciousness from a dream.

Gay, who was a carpenter and drywall hanger until four years ago, when he sold his first novel at the age of 57, is blessedly unschooled. He may do a few things writers learn not to do in workshops—such as pile on adverbs—but his prose is as natural and pure as it comes. "You got a look about you like you don't care whether you live or die, and maybe you'd a little rather die," says one character. This is fiction at its most real.

—Susannah Meadows, *Newsweek*, November 18, 2002

The author was given a small space—fewer than 350 words—in which to critique this book. Her review is compelling because it:

- Contains a clearly stated point of view, backed up by an example.
- Describes the type of writing and storytelling technique used.
- Contains plot and character description.
- Tells where the action takes place.
- Provides information about the author and his background.
- Points out a flaw (overuse of adverbs) to ground an otherwise glowing review.

KEEP THINGS OBJECTIVE

Try to learn the difference between what's objective and what's your own personal taste. Leave out the stuff that's your own taste.

MUSIC REVIEWS

If you asked 10 people to explain what constitutes good music, you'd get 10 different answers. Musical tastes vary greatly, especially among different age groups and people with different backgrounds. As a result, it is critical to know your audience when writing a review; you're writing to them specifically even though your review should be understandable to a wider audience. If your audience is high school students, you would be expected to look at rock, hip-hop, and dance music, because that's what those students listen to. If you wanted to review a classical piece, that would be fine as well—as long as your writing addressed the fact that few high school students are interested in the genre.

A music reviewer is like a juror: You must render a verdict based solely on evidence—not on preconceived ideas. If you're a huge Eminem fan, you must be open to writing a review that states how disappointing his newest CD is—if that's indeed the case. Likewise, if you can't stand his music, you shouldn't volunteer to review his new CD unless there's a legitimate chance you might like it.

Try to find a creative way to explain your reaction to the music. Don't say, "The first song was better than I expected." Be more specific. "Unlike the group's last CD, which was filled with uninspiring ballads, its newest release crackles with energy, from the opening track's screeching guitar intro to the final song's soaring vocals."

As with other types of reviews, a music review should be descriptive. That's a challenge, since it can be difficult to describe sound. But with practice, it's something that can be overcome. For starters, read other reviews from respected publications—especially reviews of music you're familiar with. Second, ask yourself many questions while listening to the music, questions that will help you find words to describe it. Be patient. It may take some time.

- How would you describe the vocals? Soft, raspy, harsh, delicate, soaring, ear-splitting?
- How would you describe the drumming? Pounding, delicate, jarring, lightning-quick?
- How would you describe the guitar playing? Thumping, strumming, wailing, booming?

Aside from the identifying characteristics about the band, such as the instruments being played and whether the singers work well together, here are some other questions to consider:

- Are the lyrics unique or are they clichéd? Do the lyrics tell a story?
- Is the music a departure from what the band has done before? If so, is this new direction a good thing? If not, is the band stagnating?

- Who might have been the musical influence for this band?
- What are the strengths and weaknesses of this music?
- How does the music make you feel?

Read the review below and note how it draws you into the group's music:

Britain's Cat in the Hat

D amon Gough, a.k.a. Badly Drawn Boy, is going to get this song right if it kills him. He's started and stopped three times so far, and he'll start and stop 12 more if that's what it takes. So what if there are 1,000 people watching him? There's a screeching buzz in his ear—sound problems, apparently—and it's not going away. "I'm sorry," he tells the crowd at Manhattan's Roseland Ballroom, "but this is the most important song off the new record." It is mid-October and Gough's third CD, "Have You Fed the Fish?" doesn't come out for a month. His fans are hearing the new material for the first time, so the sound problems are driving Gough to the brink of a snit. "I promise you," says the squat, shaggy 32-year-old in a blue knit cap, "this is one of the top five songs ever written"— pause—"by Badly Drawn Boy."

On take No. 5, Gough finally nails it, and it's worth the wait. "You Were Right," a galloping, bittersweet confessional, really is one of the top five songs ever written by Badly Drawn Boy. And that's saying something. Ever since the Manchester, England, native won Britain's Mercury Prize for his 2000 debut, "The Hour of Bewilderbeast," his refreshingly unironic sound has beguiled critics on both sides of the Atlantic. On "You Were Right," Gough wonders aloud just how much it's fair to expect from music—a fraught subject for any singer—and how fatherhood changed him more than any song ever did. (His girl, Edie, is 2; Oscar Bruce—as in Springsteen, Gough's idol—is 8 months old.) "Songs," he half-whispers, "are never quite the answer/ Just a soundtrack to a life."

"Have You Fed the Fish?"—the title refers to a phrase uttered daily in the Gough household—is a splendid mess of an album, like a packed subway car where everyone fits but a bit more room would help. Which is why it's only the *second* best Badly Drawn Boy CD of the year. Gough's soundtrack for the Hugh Grant film "About a Boy," released in the spring, is just about perfect: simple, sincere, all heart. They give out Oscars for those, don't they?

This double dose of Badly Drawn Boy has propelled Gough to monster stardom in Britain, where his furry face graces the cover of just about every music magazine. (Over here, "Fish" sold 10,000 copies in its first week.) Gough's wool knit cap has already achieved mythic status in England, having been stolen right off his head three times. "The last time it was never returned," he says. "The next day the *Sun* called and said, 'We've been sent a photograph of somebody wearing a black mask and your hat.'The way I look at it, if I never write another song, at least I made an article of clothing famous." Look at it however you want, Damon. Just keep writing songs.

—Devin Gordon, *Newsweek*, November 25, 2002

Why does this review succeed? Among other things, it transports us to a music club and we are immediately drawn in. And it has a clear point of view about the merits of the artist's work. Additionally, it:

- Tells us details about Badly Drawn Boy
- Provides insight into the lyrics
- Describes his songs ("galloping, bittersweet confessional")
- Reflects on the CD's level of originality ("refreshingly unironic")
- Targets the audience. By recognizing that most people in America have not likely heard of this artist, the reviewer explains his appeal in England.

> ### WRITE A REVIEW FOR ALMOST ANYTHING
>
> Take what you learn in this chapter and apply it to almost anything: art, architecture, a new shopping mall, a bus route, or even a college class. The key is to be objectively descriptive and to supply opinion that's backed up with details and description.

FILM/TV REVIEWS

Film and TV reviews incorporate the same writing components as do book and music reviews, but in this case, you are describing pictures and acting. That means you're dealing with a different set of criteria.

Film is considered one of our nation's grandest forms of entertainment. As a result, major movies are subject to scrutiny that few TV shows receive. Film reviews receive more prominent "play" than any other type of review, perhaps because moviegoers expect so much when they go to the cinema. With much larger budgets than TV shows, films are typically subject to greater scrutiny.

Here are some questions to keep in mind when reviewing a TV show or movie:

- What is the storyline? How is it developed?
- Is the movie successful within its genre? If it's a comedy, for instance, is it funny?
- What is the quality of the performances? Are the actors well cast in their roles?
- Is the screenwriting and dialogue strong, intelligent, and believable?

Additionally, the questions below are likely to be addressed in movie reviews:

- What's the quality of the cinematography?

- How much money was spent making the film?
- Is the director's vision for the movie clear?

Read the movie review below and note how much information it imparts:

Mood 'Ring'

"The Ring" starts like a "Scream" knockoff, with two teen-age girls creeping each other out with the tall tale of a lethal videotape: once you watch it, your phone rings and a voice tells you you have seven days to live. We soon find out it's no legend, and Gore Verbinski's horror movie—a Hollywood remake of the immensely popular 1998 Japanese movie "Ringus," which spawned two Japanese sequels—shifts into solemn gear and starts to raise some serious goose bumps. You know the movie is going to be stylish from the videotape itself, which you watch through the eyes of reporter Rachel Keller (Naomi Watts), the aunt of one of four teenagers who died a week after watching the tape. A disturbing black-and-white surrealist nightmare—filled with blood, severed fingers, centipedes and a woman hurling herself off the edge of a cliff—the video's images will supply the clues Rachel must follow as she rushes against time to save herself, her ex (Martin Henderson) and her strange, sixth-sensible son (David Dorfman) from a horrible end. This demonic ghost story is stronger on mood than character. The more the mysterious pieces fall into place, the less sense "The Ring" makes. But most horror fans will happily sacrifice coherence and plausibility for some good otherworldly jolts. Elegantly shot by Bojan Bazelli and designed by Tom Duffield, with a chilling Hans Zimmer score, this visually stunning movie serves up generous dollops of designer creepiness.

—David Ansen, *Newsweek*, October 21, 2002

This review was clearly written with fans of the horror genre in mind. Though the film wasn't terribly coherent or believable, that doesn't detract from the overall experience. If the review had focused on the movie's shortcomings, as might be expected in a traditional drama film, it would have missed the point; such movies are about thrills, and "The Ring" delivered on that end.

DEVELOPING YOUR REVIEW

Let's say you are writing a book review. First, you'll want to provide a brief synopsis of the story (but make sure you omit the ending!). Include a quote or two as well as some description that stood out to you.

Once you have detailed the basics of the book, ask yourself:

- What is the biggest impression the book left on you?
- Did the book, or the hype surrounding the book, promise something at the start? Did it live up to that promise?
- Is the book a good value for the money?

Indeed, these are questions that any potential book-buyer would have—not just a book reviewer. This underscores your role when writing as a peer. But be clear: Your job isn't to state simply whether something is good or bad, it is to describe the advantages and shortcomings that one should anticipate.

How Did We Do? Grade Us.

Thank you for choosing a Kaplan book. Your comments and suggestions are very useful to us. Please answer the following questions to assist us in our continued development of high-quality resources to meet your needs. Or go online and complete our interactive survey form at **kaplansurveys.com/books**.

The title of the Kaplan book I read was: _____

My name is: _____

My address is: _____

_____

My e-mail address is: _____

What overall grade would you give this book?   Ⓐ Ⓑ Ⓒ Ⓓ Ⓕ

How relevant was the information to your goals?   Ⓐ Ⓑ Ⓒ Ⓓ Ⓕ

How comprehensive was the information in this book?   Ⓐ Ⓑ Ⓒ Ⓓ Ⓕ

How accurate was the information in this book?   Ⓐ Ⓑ Ⓒ Ⓓ Ⓕ

How easy was the book to use?   Ⓐ Ⓑ Ⓒ Ⓓ Ⓕ

How appealing was the book's design?   Ⓐ Ⓑ Ⓒ Ⓓ Ⓕ

What were the book's strong points? _____

How could this book be improved? _____

Is there anything that we left out that you wanted to know more about?

Would you recommend this book to others?   ☐ YES   ☐ NO

Other comments: _____

_____

_____

Do we have permission to quote you?   ☐ YES   ☐ NO

Thank you for your help.
Please tear out this page and mail it to:

Managing Editor
Kaplan, Inc.
888 Seventh Avenue
New York, NY 10106

KAPLAN

Thanks!